RISING STARS
Vocabulary

Teacher's Guide
Over 100 fun activities to build vocabulary skills

Reception and Key Stage 1

Siobhan Skeffington
Charlotte Raby

Orders: please contact Bookpoint Ltd, 130 Park Drive, Milton Park, Abingdon, Oxon OX14 4SE. Telephone: (44) 01235 400555. Email: primary@bookpoint.co.uk.
Lines are open from 9 a.m. to 5 p.m., Monday to Saturday, with a 24-hour message answering service.
Visit our website at www.risingstars-uk.com for details of the full range of Rising Stars publications.

Online support and queries
Email: onlinesupport@risingstars-uk.com

ISBN: 978 1 5104 3176 8

Text, design and layout © 2018 Rising Stars UK Ltd

First published in 2018 by Rising Stars UK Ltd

Rising Stars UK Ltd, part of the Hodder Education Group,

An Hachette UK Company

Carmelite House

50 Victoria Embankment

London EC4Y 0DZ

www.risingstars-uk.com

Impression number 10 9 8 7 6 5 4 3 2 1

Year 2022 2021 2020 2019 2018

Author: Siobhan Skeffington and Charlotte Raby

Publisher: Laura White

Cover and text design: Julie Martin

Illustrations by Marek Jagucki (except pages 81, 82 and 93)

Editorial: Rachel Nickolds, Sarah Davies and Jennie Clifford

Typesetting: Aptara Inc.

Printed in the UK by Ashford Colour Press Ltd.

A catalogue record for this title is available from the British Library.

Acknowledgements

The Publishers would like to thank the following for permission to reproduce copyright material.

p81 "Fish" from *The Llama Who Had No Pajama*: 100 Favorite Poems by Mary Ann Hoberman. Copyright © 1951 by Mary Ann Hoberman. Reprinted by permission of Houghton Muffin Harcourt Publishing Company. All rights reserved.; p86 'Caterpillars' by Brod Bagert; p88 'The Dentist and the Crocodile' by Roald Dahl from Rhyme Stew published by Jonathan Cape Ltd and Penguin Books Ltd; by kind permission of David Higham Associates; p91 'The Weasel' by Ted Hughes from *Collected Poems for Children* by Ted Hughes with kind permission from Faber and Faber Limited; p95 Persephone and the Pomegranate Seeds by Geraldine McCaughrean first published in the UK by Orchard Books, an imprint of Hachette Children's Group, Carmelite House, 50 Victoria Embankment, London, EC4Y 0DZ.

Every effort has been made to trace all copyright holders, but if any have been inadvertently overlooked, the Publishers will be pleased to make the necessary arrangements at the first opportunity.

Contents

Reception

1 Can you follow instructions? 6
Words used for commands

2 How do we talk about size? 8
In context, fiction: Goldilocks and the Three Bears

3 How do animals move? 10
Words for movement and speed

4 How do we talk about objects we have made? 12
In context, fiction: The Three Little Pigs

5 Can we ask and answer questions? 14
Words for finding out information

6 Where is it? 16
Words to describe position

7 Which words help to tell stories? 18
In context, fiction: Jack and the Beanstalk

8 How do you feel? 20
Words to describe emotions

9 How are the fish moving? 22
In context, poetry: Fish by Mary Ann Hoberman

10 What are the characters like? 24
In context, fiction: Hansel and Gretel

11 Similar and opposite words in
nursery rhymes 26
In context, poetry: Twinkle, Twinkle, Little Star

12 How can we measure different things? 28
Words relating to growth and measurement

Year 1

13 How do we use our voices? 30
Words to describe different types of speech

14 Can we launch a rocket? 32
Words relating to space

15 How energetic do we feel? 34
Discovering new words for different states of energy

16 What is the material like? 36
Words to describe the properties of everyday things

17 How do we use -er and -est? 38
In context, fiction: The Three Little Pigs

18 Can you describe a mythical creature? 40
In context, fiction: The Book of Beasts by E. Nesbit

19 What sound does it make? 42
Sounds from science investigations

20 Who are the villains and heroes? 44
In context, fiction: Snow White and the Seven Dwarfs

21 Can we compare a fish and a duck? 46
Words relating to creatures

22 Which words describe a caterpillar? 48
In context, poetry: Caterpillars by Brod Bagert

23 What shall we choose in the playground? 50
Different movement words to describe a
children's playground

24 How do we know it is a traditional tale? 52
In context, fiction: Sleeping Beauty

Year 2

25 How many ways can you walk? 54
Words associated with movement

26 How does the poet make us laugh? 56
In context, poetry: The Dentist and the Crocodile
by Roald Dahl

27 How do you eat your food? 58
Words to describe eating

28 What happened in the fairy tale? 60
In context, fiction: Hansel and Gretel

29 How can we use descriptive words in rhymes? 62
In context, poetry: The Owl and the Pussy-cat

30 What is the weasel after? 64
In context, poetry: The Weasel by Ted Hughes

31 Which habitat? 66
Words associated with animals and habitats

32 Can you describe the landscape? 68
Words to describe geographical settings

33 How do we grow tomato plants? 70
In context, non-fiction: Life Cycles of Tomato Plants
by Siobhan Skeffington

34 What is he doing in the garden? 72
In context, poetry: The Garden by Andrew Marvell

35 Will you listen to our song about
the Great Fire? 74
Words relating to musical composition

36 What is the myth of Demeter and
Persephone? 76
In context, fiction: Persephone and the Pomegranate
Seeds by Geraldine McCaughrean

Introduction

What's included in *Rising Stars Vocabulary*?

Rising Stars Vocabulary comprises three Teacher's Guides covering Reception and Key Stage 1, Lower Key Stage 2 and Upper Key Stage 2 respectively. There are 12 units of work for each year group at Key Stage 1, and 16 units of work for each year group at Key Stage 2. Each unit of work contains a choice of varied discrete vocabulary activities to be planned across roughly a week. The activity ideas are entirely flexible and can be used in whatever way the teacher sees fit. Based around a collection of linked focus words, the children embark on fun, engaging and meaningful activities that widen and develop their vocabulary. The 'In context' units of work use a piece of fiction, non-fiction or poetry as a starting point for vocabulary work. This means that children develop their comprehension skills alongside their vocabulary. You will also see opportunities for writing provided throughout the resource. The focus words for each unit have been devised with cross-curricular and English curriculum links in mind, and the curriculum focus is outlined at the start of each unit. Therefore, although they are standalone activities, you can link them to your wider work where possible, should you choose to.

Activity types

As you use the series, you will become acquainted with the activity types used within it. Often we have kept to similar activity structures, such as 'Shades of meaning' and 'Act it out'. This is intentional so that children do not spend lots of time learning how to do the activity, but can dive straight into the words. This is helpful as the sessions are intended to be short and effective.

You will see the 'Act it out' activities within boxes in the units. They are particularly active activities where children use drama or role-play to learn and apply new vocabulary. The 'Word wise challenge' activities offer opportunities for children to apply their new words in writing, in a research activity or to extend the work for the more able children in the class. Home-school links are offered in the 'Words at home' boxes, that appear in units where relevant. This means that children explore the vocabulary and practise its use in the home environment.

Resources

Each of the units includes a front-of-class PowerPoint, which contains everything needed to deliver the activities within that unit. The first two slides consist of focus words and definitions for display, followed by any extracts, images, drag-and-drop activities or questions from the teaching notes. Reference to the PowerPoint is clearly indicated within the teaching notes. The PowerPoints are entirely editable for teachers to change to suit their cohort. They can be downloaded from the My Rising Stars website at www.risingstars-uk.com.

As well as the PowerPoints, there may be additional resources available for some units. Any worksheets referenced in the teaching notes can also be downloaded from My Rising Stars. All extracts are in the Teacher's Guides (for Reception and Key Stage 1 they are photocopiable for teachers) as well as on the PowerPoints for display. They can be photocopied from the book or, again, downloaded from My Rising Stars. All focus words are available as word cards to cut up and use within the activities. All equipment and resources required for the unit is listed in the 'You will need' box underneath the list of focus words.

Progression

The words and phrases for Reception, Year 1 and Year 2 have been chosen because they are slightly above the normal vocabulary range for children aged 4–7. They have just enough challenge to stretch most children and ensure that they are making new connections between familiar words and new words.

Many words have more than one meaning, and so they may appear more than once. Children learn language through repeated exposure, and words that have many meanings need to be learned over time. It can be confusing to learn all the nuances of a word's definition at once. We have tried hard to link the words clearly to a context that helps the children cement each word to its meaning within that context.

It is important to note that the emphasis of this programme is about the *meaning* of words, not spelling. Many of the words are tricky to spell, but children can still use them in their speech, recognise them in their reading and, in time, include them in their writing.

If you have children who are finding the level of the words in the units too hard, consider looking at previous units.

Tracking words taught

Research has proven that repeated use of previously taught words is crucial in moving language into children's expressive vocabularies. Use the words in this book in class to keep them alive! If the children do not have secure understanding of a word, use the activities described in the book to refresh their knowledge. Make sure you use the words that you have studied in class. Challenge the children to use the words when they talk and write.

Refer to the words you have taught (all listed in the Glossary) when you are marking writing to see which words have become part of your pupils' expressive vocabulary. Independent application of vocabulary is the real test, and repeated exposure is the key to creating a wide-ranging vocabulary.

Can you follow instructions?

Words used for commands

Words in this unit

Focus words
first
then
get
put
next
finally

You will need:

- RS Vocabulary Reception Unit 1 PowerPoint (available online at My Rising Stars)

For the jam sandwiches:
- Bread
- Butter
- Jam
- Knife
- Plate

For activity 2:
- Playground
- Beebot (optional)

In a nutshell

In Reception, the children need to learn to follow instructions so that they can become more independent inside and outside the classroom. This unit offers teachers a range of ideas to familiarise the children with the language of instructions. They start with simple instructions, such as putting on their coats and sitting on the carpet, before moving on to more difficult ones, such as making jam sandwiches.

> ### Curriculum focus:
>
> **ELG Communication and language: Understanding**
> - children follow instructions involving several ideas or actions
>
> **ELG Physical development: Moving and handling**
> - children show good control and co-ordination in large and small movements

1 Meet the words

The children first meet the following words used in simple classroom instructions: *first, then, get, put, next, finally*.

Start simply and put emphasis on the vocabulary you would like the children to learn. Model the instructions to begin with, pausing after using each of the focus words.

E.g. at play time: *First*, *get* your coat. *Then*, *put* it on. *Finally*, line up at the door.

2 Explore meaning

Explain that these words are used to help us follow instructions; *first, then, get, put, next* and *finally* tell us what to do. Words are used to explain what we want or how we are feeling, and the more words or vocabulary we use, the more easily other people will be able to understand us.

You can use these instructional words for a range of classroom activities.

Sitting on the carpet: *First*, find your place. *Then*, sit with your legs crossed.

Lining up for assembly: *First*, get behind a child in the line. *Then*, make sure you have your lips together.

3 Play with words

To extend the vocabulary of instructions, make a jam sandwich in groups. Beforehand, while washing your hands, use the vocabulary learned so far to remind the children to do the following.

- First, *put some soap on your hands.*
- Then, *rub your hands together.*
- Next, *get some water on them.*
- Finally, *dry your hands on the towel.*

The children say which words clearly told them what they needed to do and which words told them the order in which to do it. Although other verbs are used in this activity, the focus words that tell you what to do are only *get* and *put*.

Moving on to the sandwich-making, remember to keep your language simple and do not elaborate. Emphasise the key vocabulary words as you are saying them.

- First, *get a slice of bread.*
- Next, *put butter on.*
- Then, *put jam on.*
- Finally, *cut your bread in the middle.*
- Put *it on a plate and eat it!*

After the activity, ask the children why you used the emphasised words (in Roman).
The answer is that they tell us what to do and the order in which to do it.

 ## Deepen understanding

Activity 1: Simon Says

Use the game Simon Says to consolidate knowledge of how to follow a command/instruction. The children only follow the command if it starts with 'Simon says', otherwise they are out! So they must pay attention to the instruction. Use the following commands to practise the focus words.

- *Simon says* put *on your jumper.*
- Put *on your hat.*
- *Simon says* get *a book.*
- Put *your finger on your nose.*
- *Simon says* put *your hand on your head.*

Make the commands more complicated, using different verbs, as the children understand more language.

- *Simon says pat your tummy, swing your arms.*
- *Simons says walk to the door, skip to the tree.*

Challenge the children to make up a Simon Says command. Remind them that they should only follow the instruction if it begins with 'Simon says'.

Activity 2: Act it out

This activity provides the class with a more physical vocabulary session. The children could work in mixed-ability pairs or some children could be paired with additional staff. In the playground, in pairs, the children give each other instructions, which their partner listens to and follows. You could start this activity by programming beebots in pairs, before having the children programme each other as though they are robots (but using words instead of buttons!). E.g. *First, walk two paces …Then, stretch your arms … Next, jump up and down … Finally, walk back two paces.* This session may be used to assess or consolidate knowledge.

Word wise challenge

This is an opportunity for the children to use what they have learned so far and apply it with an independent (but supported) task. The children think of an instruction they could give to the teacher that uses all the focus words in this unit. Choose a simple activity such as reading a story at the end of the day. A teaching assistant could support some groups, with more able children suggesting instructions including the words *next* and *finally*. It's worth noting, when making observations for the EYFS profile, which vocabulary the children are using in order to assess how their spoken language is developing.

Words at home

The children play Simon Says at home with their parents/carers/ siblings. Can they make up their own game and decide which instructions to use? The children might share their experiences when they return to the classroom.

2 How do we talk about size?

In context, fiction: Goldilocks and the Three Bears

Words in this unit

Focus words
small
huge
tiny
large
big
smaller
larger

You will need:

- RS Vocabulary Reception Unit 2 PowerPoint (available online at My Rising Stars)
- *Goldilocks* song (see page 78 and PowerPoint available online at My Rising Stars)
- Ensure that the children know the story of *Goldilocks* - show the story or picture book while you are singing the song. There is a version on the PowerPoint if you don't have one.
- Classroom props (different-sized bowls, chairs, beds, books, cups, and so on)
- RS Vocabulary Reception Unit 2 'Different sizes' worksheet (available online at My Rising Stars)

In a nutshell

In Reception, the children should be exposed to a variety of songs and stories. This unit uses the established tale of *Goldilocks and the Three Bears* to generate a range of language activities, focusing on words that describe size. By the end of this unit, the children should be able to identify and describe objects relating to their size, and many will be able to use vocabulary to compare different sizes.

> **Curriculum focus:**
>
> **ELG Mathematics: Shape, space and measures**
> - children use everyday language to talk about size to compare quantities and to solve problems
>
> **ELG Communication and language: Listening and attention**
> - children listen attentively in a range of situations

1 Meet the words

The children meet the words in this unit when they learn the *Goldilocks* song (p78). Teach it to the children, exaggerating your own movements to indicate the size of the bowls, chairs and beds. Extend your arms for *huge* and nearly close your hands for *tiny*.

- Sing the song to the class, using movements to show the size.
- Ask the children to sing it back to you at least three times, until they are familiar with it and the story of *Goldilocks* (you can refer to the version on the PowerPoint online at My Rising Stars here if you wish). Like you, they should also use movements to represent the different sizes.
- Sing again, this time using simple props from a home corner/doll's house showing different-sized bowls, chairs and beds.

2 Explore meaning

Explain that words help us to compare different sizes. We can imagine how *big* or *small* something is by the words used to describe it. First, think about the words *huge* and *tiny*.

- Ask the children to close their eyes and picture something *huge* (e.g. a mountain, a tower, a jumbo jet plane).
- Can they show the word *huge* using their bodies, e.g. by extending their arms, going onto tiptoes or rounding their arms to make themselves appear wider? It is important that the children do not attempt to act out the object, but focus only on presenting the word *huge*.
- Discuss what the children imagined and how they represented it with their bodies.
- Next, the children close their eyes and picture something *tiny* (e.g. an ant, a pebble, a raisin).
- How would they show the word *tiny* using their bodies? (E.g. narrow their hands, crouch down low, scrunch up in a ball on the floor.)
- Ask the children what the difference is between *huge* and *tiny*, and discuss. Talk about the fact that opposites, such as *huge* and *tiny*, can help us make comparisons. Compare some of the objects imagined by the children.

Now talk about *small* and *large*.

- Ask the children what they think the difference is between *small* and *large*.
- As a class, make a list of all the things they think are *small*, such as a rubber, a mouse, a tennis ball.

- Next, ask them what they think is large. Write down all ideas (e.g. a bus, a horse, a building). During this conversation there might also be some comparison between the ideas of *huge* and *large*, *small* and *tiny*. Scaffold this discussion so that those children who are able can talk about the differences, although it's covered further in the 'Play with words' session in this unit.

 ## Play with words

Explain to the children that you will look at the words *tiny*, *huge*, *small* and *large*.

- Working independently or in groups, the children find four objects in the classroom that they could label with each word.
- Afterwards, they 'show and tell' the objects and the word used to label each one. E.g. a peg from a peg board for *tiny*, a pencil for *small*, a chair for *large*, a cupboard for *huge*.
- They must say why they chose the objects and why they labelled them as such.
- If any groups use incorrect labels, see if they can correct their work with a little help. More able children might peer review and help those in this situation.
- It is important to explain that everyone can choose different objects, but they can still be labelled correctly when *compared* to one another.
- You could use the fun PowerPoint activity 'How do we talk about size?' to consolidate knowledge here. With the children's help, sort the animals into *tiny*, *small*, *large* and *huge*.

 ## Deepen understanding

Remind the children that the words you are looking at describe different sizes; however, you can make further comparisons if you add the suffix **-er** to the words *small* and *large* to become *small**er*** and *larg**er***. These words may have already come up in conversation in other activities in this unit.

- Sing the *Goldilocks* song again and recap the story; this time, ask questions about who had *smaller* or *larger* objects. Questions might include the following.

  o *Who had a* larger *bowl than Mummy Bear?* (Daddy Bear.)
  o *Who had a* smaller *bowl than Mummy Bear?* (Baby Bear.)
  o *Who had a* larger *chair than Baby Bear?* (Mummy Bear and Daddy Bear.)
  o *Who had a* smaller *bed than Daddy Bear?* (Mummy Bear and Baby Bear.)

Emphasise that the **-er** ending makes comparisons between *small* and *large* objects easier.

Word wise challenge

Provide lots of play equipment for the home corner or during child-initiated play that allows the children to use and develop the focus words. Include different-sized bowls, books and cups. Ask them to make up their own song or story using the words they have been learning. They might perform it to the class. Ensure that all focus words are prominent in the setting.

Words at home

The children find four different objects at home and use the words they have learned to explain to their family or carers how they would order them. They can share their experiences when they return to the classroom. You could give them the 'Different sizes' worksheet to draw the objects on.

3 How do animals move?

Words for movement and speed

In a nutshell

This unit provides a variety of lively activities for the children to develop their knowledge of language relating to movement and speed. The children look at how different animals move and use appropriate vocabulary to describe the movement. It offers fantastic opportunities to get moving with the children and enjoy engaging physical and musical literacy activities to learn the new vocabulary.

Curriculum focus:

ELG Physical development: Moving and handling
- children show good control and co-ordination in large and small movements. They move confidently in a range of ways, safely negotiating space

ELG Understanding the world: The world
- children know about similarities and differences in relation to living things

---

1 Meet the words

The children meet the words by using their bodies to act them out. This might be used as part of a PE or dance lesson.

- Take the children to the hall or playground and ask them to find a space. Explain that you are going to say a word and they need to use their bodies to move in that way.
- Only use the words *slow* and *quick* to start with.
- Pick out a couple of the children who are moving well/differently and have them show the rest of the class.
- Ask the rest of the class why you chose them. *Why are their movements effective? Can you tell which word their movement is representing?*
- Repeat for the other focus words (*crawling, creeping, lazy, plodding*).
- Add *-ly* to slow and quick to create adverbs. The children can add them to other words to create phrases, such as *slowly crawling*, and *quickly creeping*. As an extension, make lazy into an adverb by adding *-ily*. The children might create a phrase like *lazily plodding*.

2 Explore meaning

Explain to the children that words help us describe movement. One way of looking at movement is to explore how different animals move.

- Use clips from the Internet (e.g. the BBC's *Blue Planet* or YouTube) to show animals moving in different ways. *Can you describe together how the animals are moving?*
- Now, without assistance, the children look at a different set of animals and see how they are moving, using the vocabulary they have learned so far to describe the way they move. They might be able to create a phrase or sentence such as: *the snail moves* slowly, *the squirrel moves* quickly, *the crab* crawls quickly, *the cat* creeps, *the elephant* plods and *the sloth moves* lazily.
- Allow the children to be creative (with support).

Play with words

Activity 1: Moving to music

Explain to the children that in this activity you will explore movement through sound, using musical instruments.

- Hand the children a selection of different percussion instruments. These could include a drum, a tambourine, a triangle, maracas, bells or any other improvised child-made instruments, such as shakers.
- Demonstrate that, when you say a word, you are going to make a sound with the instrument, as though it were an animal/person moving in that way.
- Ask the children which instruments best suit something moving quickly, e.g. a tambourine being shaken very fast, or finger clackers.
- Ask the children which instruments best suit something *plodding* along, e.g. a *slow* drum beat, or tapping woodblocks *slowly*.
- Do the same with all focus words in this unit.
- The other children can show they agree or disagree with the choice by putting their thumb up or down. They can then suggest something different using another instrument, or a different way to play the same one.

Activity 2: Act it out

Take the children into the hall and bring a bag with eight different classroom animals in it (ensure that they offer a variety of movement and speed). Without looking, pick out an animal and ask the children to move like it. Discuss the movements that children are making and then ask them to use the vocabulary in this unit (and any other words they know) to describe its movement and speed. Ensure that the words stay focused and don't just become descriptive language about the animal (e.g. *the elephant is heavy, the tiger is furry*).

 Deepen understanding

To deepen understanding of the focus words, you might explore the words *creeping* and *crawling* in more detail.

- Ask one of the children to demonstrate what they think *creeping* is.
- Ask another child to demonstrate what they think *crawling* is. Is there any difference?

The children may say that you can also creep about while standing up, but crawling is usually done closer to the floor.

How do we talk about objects we have made?

In context, fiction: The Three Little Pigs

In a nutshell

Stories offer great inspiration to make and create. This unit uses the traditional tale *The Three Little Pigs* to stimulate a range of activities that develop descriptive vocabulary. By the end of this unit, the children should be able to understand that materials are different. They may also understand more complex language to describe their properties, such as *fragile* and *sturdy*.

> ## Curriculum focus:
>
> ### ELG Expressive arts and design: Being imaginative
> - children represent their own ideas and thoughts through design and technology. They explore a variety of materials
>
> ### ELG Physical development: Moving and handling
> - children handle equipment and tools effectively

1 Meet the words

The children meet the words when discussing the Three Little Pigs' houses.

- Read the story of *The Three Little Pigs* to the children (p79), introducing the words *strong, weak, rough, smooth, sturdy, fragile*.
- Ask the class what they think each word means. Write down their answers and clarify any misconceptions.
    - **strong** – powerful/not easily broken
    - **weak** – delicate
    - **rough** – bumpy
    - **smooth** – flat
    - **fragile** – breakable
    - **sturdy** – stable
- Read the story again, pausing after the wolf blows down the house made of straw. Ask the children which of the words they would use to describe this house, and why (*weak* or *rough* – some may say *fragile*).
- Continue the story and repeat this activity for the house made of bricks (*strong* or *sturdy* – some may say *smooth*).
- Once they have explained their focus word choices, discuss how different objects can be made from different materials.

2 Explore meaning

Explain that words help us describe different materials. Tell the children that they are going to make the pigs' houses and then describe them using the new vocabulary.

- Read the story of *The Three Little Pigs* (p79) again using your classroom farm set to show the children the 'three little pigs', for context.
- Ask them to work in groups of no more than four (some may be supported by a teaching assistant/teacher) to build a house for the pigs.
- Each group should use different materials (see 'You will need').
- The children first plan what they will do and then work with an adult to make their house. This could be a focused activity with one group at a time, rather than the whole class doing it at once.

© Rising Stars UK Ltd 2018.

- More than one group can make each type of house, as long as there is a house of straw, a house of sticks and one of clay (instead of bricks). You will need to collect sticks for the activity.
- As the children are making the houses, talk about whether they feel *rough* or *smooth*, *weak* or *strong*, *fragile* or *sturdy*.

As a class, review the groups' different houses.

- The children use the words *strong, weak, rough, smooth, fragile* and *sturdy* to describe another group's house.
- They carefully feel the houses. *Do they feel rough or smooth? What is the difference?*
- Ask them which pig made the best choice, and why?

 ## Play with words

Explain that you are going to look at the words *strong, weak, rough* and *smooth* in more detail.

- Sit in a circle – as you would for circle time.
- The children retell the story of *The Three Little Pigs* a sentence at a time, but only when they have the *class prop* that lets them speak (this could be a stone, a teddy, a carved object).
- When they get to the part about the houses, they should add something about the material it is made from – is it *strong, weak, rough* or *smooth* (some may wish to use *fragile* or *sturdy*). Allow the children to extend and create descriptions using their knowledge of the story and the new vocabulary.

Ask a teaching assistant to make careful observations of the language used for assessment purposes. Pick up any misconceptions and emphasise what each word means.

 ## Deepen understanding

Make it clear that some of the words in the list mean roughly the same thing, particularly in the context of the story of *The Three Little Pigs*. For instance, a house that is *strong* can also be described as *sturdy*. A house that is *weak* might also be described as *fragile*.

- Challenge the children to build something that could be *fragile* or *sturdy* using classroom resources such as interlocking plastic bricks, plastic or wooden building blocks, connecting loops, paper, scissors and beads.
- This could take place during child-initiated play, and observations of language used should be recorded. The children could work alone, with a partner or in a small group.
- Once finished, the children describe what they have built using any of the words learned in this unit. They may need to be prompted to be more creative and not just recreate the houses!
- Finally, ask them if their structure is *fragile* or *sturdy*, and what makes it so.

Word wise challenge

Provide an area where the children can play with their houses, and use the farm animals. While there, ask them to tell the story in their own words, and change it if they want to, using the words they have learned.

Words at home

Ask the children to bring in a picture of something that is *strong, weak, rough, smooth, sturdy* or *fragile*. It could be from a newspaper or magazine, an old photo or anything they can find. Make a collage display of the pictures with captions underneath written by the children, teacher or teaching assistant.

5 Can we ask and answer questions?

Words for finding out information

Words in this unit

Focus words

why
what
how
when
can
did
where
who

You will need:

- RS Vocabulary Reception Unit 5 PowerPoint (available online at My Rising Stars)
- An interesting 'show and tell' object
- A bag containing cut up focus word cards (available online at My Rising Stars)
- A parent/carer who is willing to talk to the class about their job

In a nutshell

The children should develop their understanding of asking and answering different types of questions. This unit offers activities for the children to use questions in order to find out information. By the end of this unit, the children will show awareness of how to ask and answer questions, as well as understanding how questions differ from statements.

> ### Curriculum focus:
>
> **ELG Communication and language: Understanding**
> - children can answer 'how' and 'why' questions about their experiences and in response to stories or events
>
> **ELG Communication and language: Speaking**
> - children express themselves effectively, showing awareness of listeners' needs

1 Meet the words

Begin by discussing with the children which words begin questions. Allow time for them to come up with their own questions and think about how they might be answered.

- Start by modelling a simple 'show and tell' activity reminding the children to put their hands up to take turns.
- Show the class an interesting object such as a lovely shell, a meteorite or a fossil.
- Ask a teaching assistant to model how to ask a question using one of the focus words. Write a list of questions beforehand so that the teaching assistant has an example for each word.
- The class thinks of a question beginning with the same word, e.g. Why *did you choose to bring in that shell?* Where *did you find it?* How *many shells do you have at home?*
- Do this with the other focus words until the children are confidently using them.
- Model how you would answer using full sentences, e.g. *I found the shell on the beach.*

2 Explore meaning

Explain that we use question words to find out information. Asking a question is different to saying a statement, which gives information.

- Remind the children of one of the questions from your modelled 'show and tell': Why *did you choose to bring in that shell?* If you answered with *I like shells,* ask: *Is that a question or a statement?* (Statement.)
- Show them a different object and ask them to think of a question using one of the question words. They then answer with a statement.
- Read out a list that includes both questions and statements. Ask the children to put a thumb up if they think it is a question and down if they think it is a statement. Examples: What *is your name? I am four years old.* What *did you eat for breakfast? I walked to the park. We went shopping on Saturday.*
- Address any misconceptions by carefully explaining the difference between a statement and a question. A question is used to find out information and begins with one of the question words. A statement gives the information. Another child might also be able to explain this to those who are struggling.

14　　　　　© Rising Stars UK Ltd 2018.

It is a good idea to make a rota for 'show and tell', and have it each day or week. Children love it and it helps develop question and answer skills. Notify parents/carers when it is their child's turn to bring something in. Ask no more than three children at a time to bring something in from home to show or have something to tell everyone. Children should answer four or five questions. Ensure a lot of children get a chance to ask a question, noting who has asked a question and who has participated in 'show and tell'.

Play with words

Activity 1: Asking questions

Do this activity during child-initiated play. It allows the children to practise forming and asking their own questions, and is an effective assessment opportunity.

- Choose a small group of children, giving each one a card with a question word on (see the focus word cards available online at My Rising Stars), and ask them to go to another child in the class.
- They ask that child a question, starting with the word on the card, that might be related to what they are doing. (E.g. What *are you painting?* Why *did you choose the blocks?*)
- At the end of the session, the children report back what they asked and how the children answered.
- Perform the activity with different groups on different days.

Activity 2: Act it out

Do some 'hot seating' in class. Pretend to be a character from a story you have read recently, such as *Hansel and Gretel*. The children find out who you are by asking questions. Once they have found out, they can ask you another question about that character. Encourage different children to play the hot-seat character as they become more confident at asking and answering questions.

Deepen understanding

Explain that you have a visitor coming in who will tell them a little bit about themselves. The children will be able to ask questions.

- Ask a parent/carer to come in and talk about their job – or ask another member of staff.
- From a bag containing all the question words (available online at My Rising Stars), pick one out and ask the children to think of a question to ask starting with that word.
- At the end, ask the children if they would like to ask their questions, reminding them to put their hands up to take turns.

Words at home

At home, the children ask their parents/carers/siblings three questions and listen carefully to the answers. The next morning, as you do the register, each child says one of the questions and how their parent/carer/sibling answered.

6 Where is it?

Words to describe position

In a nutshell

In Reception, the children need to learn how to use positional language. This unit offers a range of ideas to enable the children to develop an understanding of words used to describe where something is. By the end of this unit, the children should be able to describe where something is and understand that some words mean the opposite of others.

Curriculum focus:

ELG Mathematics: Shape, space and measures
- children use everyday language to talk about position

ELG Communication and language: Understanding
- children follow instructions involving several ideas or actions

---

1 Meet the words

The children meet the words when you give instructions that they must follow. These instructions include positional language.

- Remind the children they need to follow instructions.
- Ask them to find a space in the playground (or hall) and give them an instruction using a focus word from this unit (positional language). Examples might be: *Walk two paces* forwards. *Go* around *another child. Walk* behind *someone else. Walk one step* backwards.
- Afterwards, discuss the meaning of each word to ensure that children understand them. You can ask children to show an example of each one.

2 Explore meaning

Explain to the children that they are going to follow an obstacle course. (This could be done during a PE lesson.)

- Make sure that the children are wearing appropriate clothing.
- Set up the hall or play area (ensure there is plenty of space) with mats, benches and climbing equipment (ropes, wall bars) as an obstacle course, and put the children in groups.
- Recap the meaning of the focus words in this unit if necessary.
- Ask the children to complete the obstacle course in groups: one group member at a time completes the course while the other children use the focus words to describe what that child is doing. They all take turns.

3 Play with words

Explain to the children that they are going to set up their own obstacle course for a teddy/toy.

- This should be a child-directed activity.
- Working in small groups, ask them to make an obstacle course for a teddy/toy. They could use plastic or wooden building blocks, doll's house furniture (or any classroom equipment), or make junk models in the art area.
- Then, one child takes the teddy through the course and the other children use the focus words in this unit to say what the teddy is doing.
- If available, ask one of the children to record this on a class camera or tablet; this could be played back to see if the class, as a group, can say the words.

Deepen understanding

Explain to the children that some of the words you have been looking at are opposites of each other.

- Give the children three sentences and ask which word fits best: *over* or *under*? (You could use the drag-and-drop slide on the PowerPoint here if you wish.)
    - o Fish live _____ the water.
    - o Tunnels are _____ the ground.
    - o The umbrella is _____ my head to keep the rain off.

Word wise challenge

Explain to the children that you are going to play Simon Says in the playground. Remind the children they only need to follow the instruction if it starts with 'Simon says'. Say each of the focus words, some with and some without, e.g. *Simon says move* backwards *four paces. Go* under *the awning*.

Words at home

If they have a pet, ask the children to describe what it is doing, using the focus words from the lesson, e.g. *The cat is walking* towards *its bowl*. If they don't have a pet then they could describe animals they see when they are out and about, e.g. birds, cats and dogs.

Which words help to tell stories?

In context, fiction: Jack and the Beanstalk

In a nutshell

In Reception, the children are exposed to a variety of texts, but traditional tales are particularly popular and effective as teaching resources. This unit uses *Jack and the Beanstalk* as a prompt for a variety of sessions that develop understanding of words and their meanings within the context of a story. By the end of this unit, the children should be able to use focus words appropriately and relative to their meaning, and be aware of some of their synonyms.

> **Curriculum focus:**
>
> **ELG Communication and language: Listening and attention**
> - children listen attentively in a range of situations. They listen to stories, accurately anticipating key events and respond to what they hear with relevant comments, questions or actions
>
> **ELG Expressive arts and design: Being imaginative**
> - children represent their own ideas, thoughts and feelings through role-play and stories

Meet the words

Children meet the words by listening to them in the context of the story.

- Read the story of *Jack and the Beanstalk* (p80) to the children.
- Read the story again, explaining that you want the children to listen carefully for the following words: *magic, tricked, problem, beautiful, enormous, chopped*. (You may also want to include the words *suddenly* and *strange*, depending on your cohort.) As you read the story, emphasise those words to help the children.
- Afterwards, ask the class to tell you what each of the words means and address any misconceptions. It is important that they understand meaning both in the context of this story and more generally.

Definitions
- **magic** – something that doesn't normally happen; you can't explain it
- **tricked** – someone has played a joke on you (past tense)
- **problem** – an issue that needs addressing
- **beautiful** – something enjoyable to experience
- **enormous** – very large
- **chopped** – cut something down (past tense)
- **suddenly** – something happens quickly
- **strange** – unfamiliar, unusual, odd

Explore meaning

Children explore meaning when you replace the focus words with others. They must determine whether the new word means the same thing or the opposite.

- Reread the story but this time replace the focus words with words that are either similar to the original or completely different.
- When you get to the new words, use a different voice to alert the children.
- The children need to give a thumbs-up if they think it is similar in meaning, or thumbs-down if they think it means the opposite. Model an example if you need to.

Suggested replacements

strange – funny	**problem** – puzzle	**chopped** – cut
magic – baked	**beautiful** – ugly	**suddenly** – slowly
tricked – fooled	**enormous** – small	

- Afterwards, discuss their answers and why they put their thumbs up or down.

 Play with words

In this session you model retelling the story, using alternative vocabulary to be creative. You can use the classroom equipment outlined in the 'You will need' box.

- With the children sitting in a circle, read the story and ask them to spot any words you have changed, but only once you have finished.
- Use synonyms for the focus words and see if the children can pick them out.
- Be creative by adding and changing things in the story; this models that it is good to be creative and to play with language and meaning.

 Deepen understanding

Now it's the turn of the children to retell the story, as you did in the 'Play with words' session.

- Use this activity in child-initiated play.
- Provide the children with lots of play equipment and ask them to retell the story in their own words.
- Ask a teaching assistant to observe the language being used during story-telling to assess language development.
- The story may evolve and change during the retelling. This is absolutely fine and to be encouraged.

8 How do you feel?

Words to describe emotions

In a nutshell

It is essential that the children learn to recognise, verbalise and express different emotions. This unit provides a variety of sessions where the children can talk about and show how they feel. By the end of this unit, the children should have a good understanding of what the different focus words mean and how to recognise different emotions in themselves and others.

> ### Curriculum focus:
>
> **ELG Personal, social and emotional development: Managing feelings and behaviour**
> - children talk about their own feelings
>
> **ELG Communication and language: Understanding**
> - children follow instructions involving several ideas

1 Meet the words

The children meet the words when you act out a feeling and they try to guess the emotion.

- Say to the children: *I am feeling … can you guess the feeling by seeing what my face and body are doing?*
- They can call out what they think as a group (e.g. *angry, happy*).
- Repeat for the other focus words in this unit.
- Don't tell the children which emotion each mime was until the very end, when you can go through them all and discuss how they knew the feeling. E.g. What made them realise that the word was *happy*? Were there any words that they didn't know?

2 Explore meaning

Activity 1: I feel …

Explain to the children that, together, you are going to explore different feelings during circle time.

- Ask the children to sit in a circle and pass around an object.
- When each child holds the object, they say: *I feel* angry *when …, I feel* happy *when …,* going through each of the words. They can choose one word or all, depending on time.
- Discuss as a group.

Activity 2: Morning expression

Get a set of feeling cards (available within the Focus word cards online at My Rising Stars) showing different emotions with the focus word written underneath. Stick these on to the board.

- Ask the children to stick their photograph (or name badge or tag) underneath the feeling they had that morning.
- Hopefully, everyone will have a happy face, but any other emotion can be acknowledged here.
- Discuss together, looking at the pictures and faces. E.g. *Paul is feeling* sad *because … Hani is feeling* surprised *because … Ali is feeling* angry *because …*
- This is often a good way to diffuse situations and aid communication.

Play with words

Activity 1: Guess the emotion

Explain to the children that they are going to work in pairs.

- One child acts out an emotion from the focus word list (e.g. *angry, grumpy*) and the other child has to guess which one it is.
- They then swap over.
- Ask them to stop after around three swaps (or time the activity).
- Choose a pair to demonstrate what they have been doing. Can the class guess the emotion?

Activity 2: Act it out

Now working as a class, ask the children to act out someone who is *angry*. How do they show their feelings with their body language? What kind of things might they say? Use a large area for free movement. Act out all the different focus words and together discuss the movements used.

Deepen understanding

Tell the children that you are now going to look at how the words relate to one other.

- Explain that you are going to make a word line together.
- Hang a piece of string across the classroom and print out the focus words (available online at My Rising Stars).
- Ask: *If we start with* happy *at one end, what is the opposite that should go at the other end? Where should the other words be placed, and why?*
- Encourage discussion about how more negative words, such as *sad, angry, grumpy* and *worried*, might go together and positive words, such as *happy* and *amused*, might go together.
- Ask the children what they think the focus word, *embarrassed* means. Does it make them feel good or bad? *Where would it fit on the word line?*
- Then discuss where *surprised* could go. *Could it go on either side?*
- Arrange the words in the order the children think they should go, following lots of discussion.

Words at home

Send home a picture of the class word line. Explain to the children that you would like them to talk this through with their parents/carers or siblings to see if they agree or would change any of the words, and why. Share experiences with the class the following day and make any changes to the word line as a result.

9 How are the fish moving?

In context, poetry: Fish by Mary Ann Hoberman

Words in this unit

Focus words
flit
racing
swerving
curving
scurrying
chasing
tearing
leap
bound

You will need:

- RS Vocabulary Reception Unit 9 PowerPoint (available online at My Rising Stars)
- The poem *Fish* by Mary Ann Hoberman (see page 81 and PowerPoint available online at My Rising Stars)
- Water tray with toy fish
- Internet clip of fish swimming

In a nutshell

In Reception, the children will be developing their understanding of more complex descriptive words. This unit offers teachers a range of ideas to enable the children to explore and play with the meaning of words in context. By the end of this unit, the children should know a variety of words that mean moving quickly, which will also help to develop comprehension skills.

> ### Curriculum focus:
>
> **ELG Communication and language: Listening and attention**
> - children listen attentively in a range of situations. They listen to stories, accurately anticipating key events and respond to what they hear with relevant comments, questions or actions
>
> **ELG Physical development: Moving and handling**
> - children show good control and co-ordination in large and small movements

1 Meet the words

Children will meet the words by listening to the poem *Fish*.

- Read the poem (p81) to the children two or three times. Ask: *What does the poem tell us the fish are doing?*
- Now read the focus words. Ask the children: *What do the focus words tell us?*
- Ask the children to close their eyes while you read the poem again. Encourage them to imagine what the fish are doing by creating a picture that they can see with their eyes closed!
- They should say the fish are moving very quickly and silently.
- Discuss how words can make pictures in your mind in this way.

2 Explore meaning

Activity 1: Meaning in context

Look at the words in more detail by discussing meaning in context.

- Read the poem again and ask the children which focus word gives them a clue that the fish are moving quickly. Some may say *racing*.
- *Are there any other words in the poem that mean 'moving quickly'?* Discuss together and list them.
- Have the children noticed three words in the list that sound different (*flit, leap and bound*)? *Why do they sound different, and how can they be made to sound the same as the others?* (They don't end with **-ing**; by adding **-ing**).

Activity 2: Move like a fish

Next, the children will explore the meaning of the movement words using physical hand actions to represent the fish.

- Say each word and ask the children to demonstrate the movement using their hands, with their palms together like a fish. The children will have lots of fun doing this!
- Model the movement and suggest a synonym (see below), or ask the children to suggest one.

- Pick out any child making a correct movement to show the other children.

Synonyms

flit – dart   **curving** – bending   **tearing** – speeding

racing – dashing   **scurrying** – hurrying   **leap** – move swiftly

swerving – zigzagging   **chasing** – following   **bound** – spring

3 Play with words

Explain to the children that you would like them to think of other words that mean moving quickly.

- Provide play opportunities with the water tray and toy fish.
- Observe their use of language and how they make their fish move.
- When they have had an opportunity to play with the water tray in groups, make a class list of all the words they can think of that mean moving quickly.

4 Deepen understanding

Explain to the children that these words could be used to describe the movements of other animals, not just fish.

- Ask the children to think about which other animals could make these movements (e.g. crocodiles, cheetahs, cats, wolves) and make a list together.
- Work together to decide which movements each animal could make. Think why some movements do not match different animals, e.g. a snail can't scurry because it doesn't have any feet!
- The children answer 'yes' or 'no' to these questions.

Can an elephant scurry?   *Can a whale* tear *about?*

Can a dragonfly flit?   *Can a worm* chase?

Can a lioness swerve?   *Can a monkey* leap?

Can a snake curve?   *Can a snail* bound?

Word wise challenge

Show an Internet clip of fish moving about and ask the children to use the words they have been focusing on to describe the fish. Ask them to use full sentences, such as: *The blue fish is* scurrying *across the rock.* You may need to model first.

Words at home

Ask the children to tell a parent/carer as many words as they can remember that mean moving quickly. Take a quick tally after the weekend by getting the children to stand up and then sit down if they remembered one word, two words, etc.

What are the characters like?

In context, fiction: Hansel and Gretel

Words in this unit

Focus words
foolish
cruel
selfish
brave
wicked
lazy
nasty
kind

You will need:

- RS Vocabulary Reception Unit 10 PowerPoint (available online at My Rising Stars)
- A version of the story *Hansel and Gretel* (see page 82 and PowerPoint available online at My Rising Stars)
- Well-stocked dressing-up area
- Focus words pinned up in the dressing-up area

In a nutshell

In Reception, the children will be listening to a variety of texts and describing lots of different characters. This unit offers teachers a range of ideas to enable the children to develop an understanding of words to describe different characters. By the end of this unit, the children should know that there can be a variety of different words to describe a character.

> ### Curriculum focus:
>
> **ELG Literacy: Reading**
> - children demonstrate an understanding when talking with others about what they have read
>
> **ELG Expressive arts and design: Being imaginative**
> - children represent their own ideas, thoughts and feelings through role-play and stories

1 Meet the words

The children meet the words in context within the well-known fairy tale *Hansel and Gretel*.

- Read the story of *Hansel and Gretel* (p82) to the children and check that they understand who the main characters are.
- Ask them what the family relationships are. Can they explain who the stepmother is?
- After reading the story, say all the focus words and ask the children which of the characters each one is used to describe. Read the story more than once if required.

foolish – woodcutter	*brave* – Hansel	*lazy* – witch
cruel – stepmother	*brave* – Gretel	*nasty* – stepmother
selfish – stepmother	*wicked* – witch	*kind* – father (woodcutter)

- Some characters have more than one descriptive word to describe them. Who are they?

2 Explore meaning

Now you will look at the words in more detail and examine how they are used to describe the characters in the story.

- Ask the children, in pairs, what the word *foolish* tells us about the woodcutter. *What kind of character is he?*
- Ask random pairs to give their answer to ensure a variety of children are answering the questions. This will also enable you to observe and assess more effectively.
- Ask the children if there is another word to describe the woodcutter. They should notice that the other word is *kind*. Discuss whether this means the same as *foolish*. Ask what else it tells us about the woodcutter. *How might the two characteristics be linked?*
- Repeat for the other words during another short session.

Play with words

The children can now have some fun with the character words as they dress up and use them to create their own stories.

- Provide a well-stocked dressing-up area for child-initiated play; the children could also make their own props.
- The children can tell their own version of *Hansel and Gretel* if they need a familiar story to work from. Otherwise, prompt and support them to make up whatever story they choose!
- More able children may develop their own story using different vocabulary, but make sure that the unit's focus words are pinned up in the area to help them describe their characters.

 ## Deepen understanding

Explain to the children that they can use these words to describe lots of different characters.

- Read the class a definition (see below and the glossary, also available online at My Rising Stars) and ask them to tell you what the word is. Explain that, for this activity, they may all call out together. Address any misconceptions.
  - **selfish** – someone who thinks about what they need rather than what anyone else needs
  - **brave** – someone who is ready to face danger or something difficult
  - **lazy** – someone who wants others to do things for them
  - **nasty** – someone who is mean or unkind
  - **kind** – someone who thinks about what other people need

Word wise challenge

What is the difference between *cruel* and *nasty*? *Cruel* means wilfully causing pain, *nasty* means behaving in an unpleasant way. They are very similar but slightly different. More able children may be able to describe how the witch is *cruel* because she locks Hansel in a cage and is *nasty* because she wants to eat him. Ask the children to write or record a description of a *cruel* or *nasty* character.

Words at home

Ask the children to read or tell a favourite story at home. Encourage them to make sure they use character words, and other descriptive words, to describe their characters.

Similar and opposite words in nursery rhymes

In context, poetry: Twinkle, Twinkle, Little Star

In a nutshell

The children listen to a variety of nursery rhymes at home and in school. This unit provides a range of activities that develop the skill of comparing words. By the end of this unit, the children should be able to say the similarities and differences between daytime and night-time and use words to describe them.

Curriculum focus:

ELG Understanding the world: The world
- children know about similarities and differences in relation to places, objects, materials and living things

ELG Literacy: Reading
- children demonstrate an understanding when talking with others about what they have read

1 Meet the words

The children meet the words when they listen and sing the two nursery rhymes.

Activity 1: Twinkle, Twinkle

Sing *Twinkle, Twinkle, Little Star* together (available on the PowerPoint online at My Rising Stars). The children will know this very well and are likely to join in with actions. Remind them that this is a nursery rhyme about night-time, specifically about the stars shining in the night sky.

- Ask the children what else is often out at night apart from the stars. (The Moon.) Ask what moonlight is, and discuss. (The world is being lit only by the Moon and the Sun has 'gone to sleep'.)
- Ask: *What do we see at night?* (Moon, stars, planets, darkness, owls.)
- Introduce the focus words related to night-time: *starlight, moonlight, high, low, shining, shiny, twinkle, sparkle, glimmer.*
- Explain that sometimes the Moon can be high or low in the sky. Ask what might be *shining* at night. (The Moon.)
- Ask what other words apart from *twinkle* could describe the stars. (*Sparkle, glimmer.*)

Activity 2: Girls and Boys

Explain that you are going to look at another rhyme.

- Read/sing the *Girls and Boys* nursery rhyme (see PowerPoint online at My Rising Stars). Read/sing it together and discuss what it is about.
- Ask the children what *sunshine* is. (The opposite of *moonlight*. During the day, the world is lit up by the Sun – when it is 'awake'.)
- Ask: *What do we see in the day?* (Clouds, blue sky, birds.)
- Introduce the focus words related to daytime: *sunshine, high, low, shining, shiny, twinkle, sparkle, glimmer.*
- Some of the words are the same because they can be used to describe both day and night. This is explored in more detail in the next session.

Explore meaning

Explain that you are going to look in more detail at the words and their meanings. This activity explores how many of the focus words can be used to describe **both** day and night.

- Remind the children of all the focus words: *starlight, moonlight, sunshine, high, low, shining, shiny, twinkle, sparkle, glimmer*.
- Make a class Venn diagram, showing interlocking circles, on sugar paper. Ask the children which words are connected with the Moon and Sun, and which could be used for both. (Both: *high, low, shining, shiny, twinkle, sparkle, glimmer*.) Write these words in the centre of the Venn diagram.
- Ask them why we use *high* and *low* for both day and night (both the Sun and Moon can appear high or low in the sky) and why we use *glimmer, shining, shiny, twinkle, sparkle* to describe the Sun and Moon (they describe how light moves).

 Play with words

Activity 1: Act it out

- Ask which of the focus words are opposites (*high/low*, *sunshine/moonlight*) and what being opposites means. Accept explanations that suggest one word is completely different to another or is the reverse of it. Can the children suggest any other words that are opposites?
- Sing *Twinkle, Twinkle, Little Star* again. Ask the children: *Where is the star?* ('High'.) Then ask them to reach up as high as they can and then bend down low. Explain that you are going to say a word; if it can be found high up they must stretch up, and if it is low they must bend down to reach the floor.
- Call out: Moon, stars, feet, planets, mud, worms, Sun.

Activity 2: Synonyms

- Now look at *glimmer, shining, shiny, twinkle, sparkle*. Explain that these words are *not* opposites: they are similar, but only slightly different.
- Ask the children, in pairs, to think of another example of something that *sparkles* (e.g. a ring or jewel). Repeat for *glimmer, shining, shiny* and *twinkle*, making a list of their ideas on the whiteboard, e.g.:

  - *A lamp might be* shining *in a dark room.*
  - *Wrapping paper is* shiny.
  - *Fairy lights* twinkle.
  - *A lake* glimmers *in the sunlight.*

 Deepen understanding

Explain that you are going to look closely at the line 'The moon is shining as bright as day' from *Girls and Boys*.

- Repeat the nursery rhyme and emphasise this line. *Does it make sense? How can it be as bright as day?*
- Some children may be able to explain that sometimes the Moon is shining so brightly it could almost be daytime.

> **Words at home**
>
> At home, the children make actions for the focus words used in the nursery rhymes. Choose some children to lead the singing or say one of the nursery rhymes and the class can learn different actions.

How can we measure different things?

Words relating to growth and measurement

Words in this unit

Focus words

grow
measure
measuring
measurement
tape measure
wide
tall
taller
small
smaller

You will need:

- RS Vocabulary Reception Unit 12 PowerPoint (available online at My Rising Stars)
- Focus words and definitions, cut up
- Tape measure
- Cups, moist cotton wool and cress
- Pots, soil, beans
- Squared paper

In a nutshell

The children are always learning how to make comparisons, and in the spring and summer terms they will be watching many things grow. This unit gives ideas for teaching children different words relating to *measurement* at this time of the year. By the end of this unit, the children will have an understanding that root words can stay the same, but suffixes can change their meaning slightly. **The children will need to plant and grow their beans before starting these activities. Beans can take 2–4 weeks to germinate, and will need planting in soil, with access to sunlight and water. Cress seeds will grow within a week.**

> ### Curriculum focus:
>
> **ELG Mathematics: Shape, space and measures**
> - children use everyday language to talk about size
>
> **ELG Understanding the world: The world**
> - children make observations of plants and explain why some things occur, and talk about changes

1 Meet the words

The children meet the words when they make comparisons between themselves, their cress and their bean plants.

- Introduce the focus words: *grow, measure, measuring, measurement, tape measure, wide, tall, taller, small, smaller*.
- Ask the children to guess why you have chosen these particular words (because we want to see how tall our plants are!) and if they know what equipment they will use to find out how tall they are (*tape measure*, ruler).
- Ask why we use *smaller* and *taller*, instead of *small* and *tall*. (Adding the **-er** suffix makes a direct comparison easier – see Unit 2.)
- Stick the cut up focus words and definitions on the board in a jumbled order for the following words: *grow, measure, wide, small, tall*.
- After discussing in pairs, choose children to come to the front of the class and join the correct word to the correct definition. Correct any misconceptions. The other children in the class can help you.
  - **grow** – to get bigger
  - **measure** – to work out the size of something
  - **wide** – describes a big distance from one edge to another
  - **small** – describes something that doesn't take up much space
  - **tall** – describes something that is high

2 Explore meaning

Explain that the children are going to *measure* themselves, their beans and their cress. They can do all three or just one of these activities.

- In groups or pairs, using a *tape measure*, the children *measure* their beans, cress and finally themselves, so they can make a comparison. Not all children will want to *measure* all three.
- If the children haven't used a *tape measure* before, model it first with a teaching assistant or a child.

- Give the children squared paper so that they can collect their results on to a block graph. Provide assistance in pairs or groups as necessary.
- Ensure they are using the focus words to complete the activity.
- Ask them: *How* tall *are you? How* tall *is your plant? Is your plant* wide?
- When you have all of the information on the graph, ask the class questions so they can make comparisons. *Is* [Ben's] *plant* taller *than* [Poppy's]*? Is* [Li] smaller *than* [Amy]*?*

 ## 3 Play with words

Explain that you are going to look further at comparisons. Ask the children the following questions. They should discuss in pairs before feeding back.

- *Which is* taller?
  - *a baby or an adult*
  - *a house or a block of flats*
  - *a dog or a horse*
  - *a tree or a flower*
- *Which* word *is better?*
  - *If I am* measuring *the teddy's tummy, am I* measuring *how* tall *it is or how* wide *it is?*
  - *If I am* measuring *you every term, will I* measure *how you* grow *or how you get* small?
  - *If the animal doesn't take up much space, is it* big *or* small?

4 Deepen understanding

Explain that you are going to look at the words *measure, measuring* and *measurement*.

- Ask what the difference is between them, explaining that all three words have the same root word but the suffixes give each one a slightly different meaning.
- Say each word and explain that *to measure* is to find out the size of something.
- Demonstrate by saying: *I am going to* measure *this pencil.*
- Explain that when you are *measuring*, you are actually taking the *measurement*. *Measure* the pencil and say: *I am* measuring *the pencil*, and finally: *I have taken a* measurement *of the pencil with the ruler.*
- Explain that the *measurement* is the number that tells you the size, e.g. the pencil you have *measured* is 10 cm long.

> ### Words at home
>
> Ask the children to find something *small, tall* and *wide* at home, and to *measure* the things they find, if they can. They could use a *tape measure* or could improvise and use another object, such as a toy car, to see how *small, tall* and *wide* their objects are.

13 How do we use our voices?

Words to describe different types of speech

Words in this unit

Focus words
whisper
yell
howl
yelp
chat
chatter
squeak
shriek
mumble
mutter

You will need:

- RS Vocabulary Year 1 Unit 13 PowerPoint (available online at My Rising Stars)
- Focus word cards displayed in the classroom – to be used in the activities (available online at My Rising Stars)
- Two cards for each child: a blue card saying 'quiet' and a red card saying 'loud' (see Focus words available online at My Rising Stars)
- Playground/hall

In a nutshell

In Year 1, the children continue to develop their vocabulary through simple comparison. This unit provides a range of activity ideas to increase understanding of words connected with speech. By the end of the unit, the children will understand that some words represent quiet speech and others loud speech. Some words can mean either.

Curriculum focus:

Spoken language
- the quality and variety of language that children hear and speak are vital for developing their vocabulary and grammar and their understanding for reading and writing
- use relevant strategies to build their vocabulary

Reading comprehension
- discussing word meanings, linking new meanings to those already known
- drawing on what they already know or on background information and vocabulary provided by the teacher

1 Meet the words

The children work in talk partners to create their own definitions of the focus words and discuss meanings.

- Display the focus words using the PowerPoint or word cards (available online at My Rising Stars), or write them on the whiteboard.
- The children discuss with a talk partner what they think the words mean. Some might create their own simple definitions.
- Choose pairs to feed back their thoughts and offer definitions, if they have them.
- Write your definition on the whiteboard/flip chart or display the PowerPoint slide of definitions (available online at My Rising Stars).
- Together, compare the children's attempts with the real definitions and address any misconceptions.

2 Explore meaning

The children consider whether the focus words represent 'quiet' or 'loud' speech.

- Ask the children to think about the sound that each word describes – is it loud, quiet or both?
- Say each word and consider together which words are spoken in a quiet voice and which in a loud voice. Sort them into two groups ('quiet' and 'loud') on the whiteboard/flip chart.
- Hand out the quiet and loud colour cards for each child (available in the Focus words online at My Rising Stars). Next, read out the sentences from the last slide (see the PowerPoint online at My Rising Stars). The children should show their red card if the focus word is 'loud' and their blue card if the focus word is 'quiet'.
- Ask the children which word could be either 'loud' or 'quiet' (*chat*), and why. If they say a different word, discuss and address any misconceptions.

Play with words

Activity 1: Act the word

- In a large playground or hall, ask the children to say each word in the same manner as you do.
- Say each word as its meaning, e.g. yell *yell*, whisper whisper, etc.
- Make a movement to show the size of the word, e.g. a large, expansive movement for *yell* and a small, huddled shape for *mutter*.
- The children say each word and make the movement with you; repeat with as many words from the list as you want to.

Activity 2: Emotions

In the classroom, look at how you might use these words, and discuss the emotions they are linked to.

- Ask the children if they think they might *yell* when they are happy. Discuss.
- How would they feel if they were *yelping*?
- Say each word and ask the children when they might use each one. Write the words on the whiteboard/flip chart.
- Sort the words into broad emotions: happy, cross, excited, scared, etc. Ask: *Could some of the words go into more than one emotion?* Discuss.

Deepen understanding

Play a game: When Would You Use This Word? This can link to the work completed in Activity 2 of 'Play with words'.

- Read out the following scenarios and ask the children if they would *yell*. They could put their thumb up if they would and their thumb down if they would not.
    - *Having fun in the playground.*
    - *In assembly.*
    - *In a crowded room to call a friend.*
    - *In the library.*
- Ask the children when they would hear a *yelp*.
    - *When someone is hurt.*
    - *If you were surprised.*
    - *If someone gave you a hug.*
    - *When a dog sees someone it doesn't know.*

Continue with as many other words and scenarios as you see fit.

Word wise challenge

Remind the children that the words *mutter, mumble* and *whisper* all describe quiet talking. Ask them how they are different. Can they give an example? Use their examples to address any misconceptions. Use the examples below if the children are having difficulty.

- The children *whispered* secrets to each other.
- Fara *mumbled* the words to the song.
- "Rats!" *muttered* the witch. "Those children have got away!"

Words at home

The children talk to their parents/carers or siblings in different ways and ask them to guess which of the focus words they are demonstrating. They should use as many of the focus words as they can remember. Choose some children to demonstrate during carpet time.

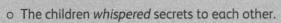

14 Can we launch a rocket?

Words relating to space

Words in this unit

Focus words

orbit
astronaut
rocket
launch
countdown
Earth
take-off
acceleration
capsule
weightlessness

You will need:

- RS Vocabulary Year 1 Unit 14 PowerPoint (available online at My Rising Stars)
- Whiteboard/flip chart
- The video of Tim Peake's rocket launch and thumbs up – search "Tim Peake's rocket launch and thumbs up - Blast Off Live: A Stargazing Special - BBC One" online
- Materials for making rockets: scissors; sticky tape; glue; long, tubular boxes from stackable crisps; cereal boxes; paper; card; egg boxes; a variety of different kinds of boxes; cloth
- Small world people
- Tablet/camera
- A list of focus words to display and to be sent home

In a nutshell

In Year 1, the children embark on practical projects that link to their wider curriculum objectives, such as science and geography. This unit allows children to learn and explore new vocabulary through the practical context of making a rocket and an exciting national event such as the space exploration of Tim Peake. By the end of this unit, the children will be able to write a short recount of an actual event using their new language.

Curriculum focus:

Spoken language
- the quality and variety of language that children hear and speak are vital for developing their vocabulary and grammar and their understanding for reading and writing
- use relevant strategies to build their vocabulary

Reading comprehension
- discussing word meanings, linking new meanings to those already known
- drawing on what they already know or on background information and vocabulary provided by the teacher

Design and technology
Design
- design purposeful and appealing products based on design criteria
- generate, develop, model and communicate their ideas through talking and drawing
Make
- select from and use a range of materials

1 Meet the words

The children will meet the words by listening to them and guessing what they relate to.

- Explain that you are going to read the list of focus words and the children should guess what they all have in common (space).
- Choose two children to say their ideas.
- Read the list of focus words again and ask the children to spot them in the video clip you are about to show them.
- Show them a clip of Tim Peake's rocket launch in December 2015; then show them the picture of weightlessness (see the PowerPoint available online at My Rising Stars).
- Ask if they spotted the focus words in the video clip, and write them on the whiteboard/flip chart.
- The children suggest their meanings. Address any misconceptions.
- It is possible to set this unit within the context of a book. Jilly Murphy's *Whatever Next* is about a bear who goes into space after building a rocket out of junk.

2 Explore meaning

Explain to the children that you would like them to look at the focus words again.

- Look at the focus words and ask the children to give you a sentence that uses some of them. They should relate to the video clip they have just seen. They can work in pairs or individually.

- Give the children time to rehearse the sentences with a partner.
- Demonstrate these two sentences first, emphasising the use of the space vocabulary.
  At the launch *Tim Peake's* rocket *was ready for* take-off.
  Tim Peake was able to float around the capsule *because there is* weightlessness *in space.*

3 Play with words

- Put the children into small groups (mixed ability, if possible).
- In groups, they design, plan and make a rocket like Tim Peake's.
- Remind them that, like Tim Peake's rocket, it will need to have a detachable capsule that can come apart when the initial launch is completed.
- Emphasise the importance of planning the rocket before making it, and give them time to do so. They can do this orally, in sentences or by drawing pictures.
- Once planning is complete, ask the children what materials they would like to use. Ensure they have everything they need to make their rocket.
- Model using the new space vocabulary when discussing, planning and making the rockets. Urge them to do the same and observe the groups as they are working.

4 Deepen understanding

The children are going to recreate Tim Peake's launch into space using their own rockets and small world people.

- In their groups, the children practise retelling the launch of Tim Peake's rocket using their own rocket and small world people.
- One child could be the narrator, ensuring that all the space vocabulary (and more if they wish!) is used to narrate what is happening.
- They can take turns to perform their *launch* to the class or, better, film/record the event on a tablet or camera and show it to the rest of the class.
- Let the children explain what they did, again modelling effective use of the space vocabulary.
- The children can peer review the performances or the videos. Did they use all the focus words correctly? How could they have used them differently? What might they change to improve? What did the children enjoy?

Word wise challenge

The children write a short recount about Tim Peake using five or more of the focus words. They can use some of the sentences used in 'Explore meaning'. Write the focus words on the whiteboard/flip chart and any other writing aids usually provided.

Words at home

Ask the children to explain in detail to their parents/carers or siblings what they have been learning about space. They should include all their focus words – send a list of them home to remind the children.

How energetic do we feel?

Discovering new words for different states of energy

Words in this unit

Focus words
tired
lively
drowsy
exhausted
bouncy
sluggish
weary
active
energetic
dynamic

You will need:

- RS Vocabulary Year 1 Unit 15 PowerPoint (available online at My Rising Stars)
- Playground/hall
- Focus word cards
- RS Vocabulary Year 1 Unit 15 'Energy Diary' worksheet (available online at My Rising Stars)

In a nutshell

In Year 1, the children become more familiar with synonyms to describe how they feel. This unit provides a range of activities where the children describe how *lively* or *tired* they feel. By the end of this unit, the children will be able to describe how they feel at different times during the day and at school.

Curriculum focus:

Spoken language
- the quality and variety of language that children hear and speak are vital for developing their vocabulary and grammar and their understanding for reading and writing
- use relevant strategies to build their vocabulary

Reading comprehension
- discussing word meanings, linking new meanings to those already known
- drawing on what they already know or on background information and vocabulary provided by the teacher

1 Meet the words

Act it out

Children act out the words in a session in the hall/playground or in a drama session.

- Ask the children to find a space in the hall or playground.
- Explain that you are going to say each of the focus words and they have to move as if they were feeling that way.
- Choose a child to demonstrate the correct way of moving in each way, e.g. *tired, bouncy, active*. If they are having any difficulties, show them how to move.
- Ask the other children to copy them and act out the focus word.
- Repeat for all the other focus words. What can they do to differentiate the words that are similar?

2 Explore meaning

Activity 1: True or false?

The children decide whether statements are true or false.

- Read the statements below to the children and ask them to show if they think they are true by putting a thumb up or false by putting a thumb down.
    - *I hop and skip about when I am* drowsy.
    - *The sprinter was* exhausted *after the race.*
    - *I am* weary *after a long walk over the hills.*
    - *The dog was* energetic. *It ran across the field and into the woods.*
    - *I am* sluggish *in the morning; it takes me ages to get dressed!*
    - *The* tired *snail slowly climbed the wall.*
    - *The* lively *boy fell asleep on his bed.*

Activity 2: Which is more *lively*?

Next, the children compare and order words, thinking about which word is more *lively*.

- Hold up two of the focus words written on cards and ask the children to call out which word is more *lively*, e.g. *sluggish* and *bouncy* (*bouncy*).
- Choose someone randomly to explain their reasoning.
- Repeat with other words that are different, such as *drowsy* and *active*.

 3 Play with words

- Ask the children:

  o *Would you rather go to a party with an* exhausted *friend or an* energetic *friend?*
  o *Would you rather feel* bouncy *at a soft-play session or* weary*?*
  o *Would you prefer to be taught by a* sluggish *teacher or a* dynamic *teacher?*

- Can they explain their choice?
- With a partner, ask the children to discuss times when they felt:

  o *drowsy*   o *sluggish*
  o *dynamic*   o *exhausted*

Encourage the children to feed back their examples. Address any misconceptions.

4 Deepen understanding

You are going to look at some of the words in a little more detail, comparing those that are similar in meaning.

- Play the game again where the children decide which word is more *lively* (see Activity 2, 'Explore meaning'), but this time they compare words that are similar.
- Ask which word is more *lively*: *sluggish* or *weary*? (*Sluggish* means slow-moving and *weary* means extremely tired.)
- Could either be considered 'livelier' than the other? Ask for their reasoning and discuss.
- Repeat for *dynamic* and *energetic*.

Word wise challenge

Ask the children to sort the words into two groups. How would they sort them and which words would they put together? All the words relating to *tiredness* should be together and all those relating to being *active* should be together. This could be done as a class activity or in small groups. The children should explain their choices.

Words at home

The children keep a record over the weekend of how they or a parent/carer/sibling feels at different times of the day (see the 'Energy diary' worksheet available online at My Rising Stars). This is to show how we all feel differently over the course of the day. We might feel *energetic* or *tired* in the morning and *drowsy* at night. They should use the focus words and share their findings with the class.

16 What is the material like?

Words to describe the properties of everyday things

Words in this unit

Focus words
stretchy
stiff
shiny
dull
bendy
not bendy
waterproof
not waterproof
opaque
transparent

You will need:

- RS Vocabulary Year 1 Unit 16 PowerPoint (available online at My Rising Stars)
- A variety of materials / objects that show different properties (e.g. stretchy, stiff, etc)
- Focus word cards, cut up
- A table to put materials and word cards on
- A table with a plastic cover, jug and bowl of water on it (to test whether material is waterproof)

In a nutshell

In Year 1 science learning, the children look at the properties of different materials. This unit provides a variety of activity ideas that experiment with different materials and explore their opposites. By the end of this unit, the children will be able to describe materials using vocabulary associated with properties.

Curriculum focus:

Spoken language
- the quality and variety of language that children hear and speak are vital for developing their vocabulary and grammar and their understanding for reading and writing
- use relevant strategies to build their vocabulary

Reading comprehension
- discussing word meanings, linking new meanings to those already known
- drawing on what they already know or on background information and vocabulary provided by the teacher

Science: Everyday materials
- describe the simple physical properties of a variety of everyday materials
- compare and group together a variety of everyday materials on the basis of their simple physical properties

1 Meet the words

Children work in small groups to explore a range of materials/objects that can be described with the focus words.

- Cut out the focus words and place all the materials on a table with their associated focus word face down.
- Place the children into small groups and ask them to look at the materials on the table. Display the focus words or provide the children with their own cut-out versions and ask them to match the material to a focus word (for the purpose of this activity, encourage the children to apply just one focus word per object). Some groups may work independently to sort the materials but some may need support from a teaching assistant or the teacher.
- When they have all sorted and discussed the materials, turn over your focus words on the table. Discuss how you sorted them, and why. Clarify any misconceptions.

2 Explore meaning

Some of the materials can be described by more than one focus word.

- In small groups, the children investigate the materials and decide which ones link to more than one word, e.g. a raincoat is *waterproof*, *opaque* and *bendy*.
- Provide an area where they can test whether materials are *waterproof* or not.
- The children choose three materials and place all the cards they can use to describe them next to each one.
- Say one of the materials and challenge the children to use as many words as possible to describe it. E.g. a still mineral water bottle is *waterproof*, *transparent* and a little bit *bendy* (if it is empty).

Play with words

Activity 1: Opposites

Some of the words are opposites.

- Call out one of the focus words and ask the children to call out the opposite word (e.g. you call out *waterproof*, the children call out *not waterproof*).
- Mix up the cards and choose a child to be the teacher. They pick a word and call it out. Their classmates must call out the opposite word correctly.

Activity 2: Have you ever …?

Now you are going to talk about experiences using materials.

- Put the children into pairs and read out the following questions in turn (you could display them on the PowerPoint if necessary).
    - *Have you ever worn something* shiny? *What was it like?*
    - *Have you ever worn a* waterproof *coat? What did it do?*
    - *Have you ever seen something* opaque? *What was it?*
    - *Have you ever looked through something* transparent? *What did you see?*
- After each question the partners must discuss their answers.
- When a pair is chosen, each partner must remember what the other has said and feed back. This tests children's listening skills as well as their knowledge of the vocabulary.

 ## Deepen understanding

Explain that you would like the children to decide whether these statements are true or false.

- Read the statements below to the children.
- If they think they are true, they put a thumb up. If false, they put a thumb down.
    - Waterproof *material makes a great raincoat.*
    - *A marshmallow is* stiff.
    - *You can see through something* transparent.
    - Dull *tinsel would be great for decorating a Christmas tree.*
    - *Milk is* opaque.
    - *A stone is* stretchy.
- Discuss answers and address misconceptions.

> **Words at home**
>
> Ask the children to find three objects at home and use their focus words to describe their properties to a parent/carer or sibling. They could bring them into class for a 'show and tell'.

How do we use *-er* and *-est*?

In context, fiction: The Three Little Pigs

You will need:
- RS Vocabulary Year 1 Unit 17 PowerPoint (available online at My Rising Stars)
- Playground/hall or large space
- Normal classroom equipment
- Strips of paper/thread/pipe cleaners of different lengths
- Story of *The Three Little Pigs* (see page 79 and PowerPoint available online at My Rising Stars)

In a nutshell

In Year 1, the children begin to use more extensive comparative language. This unit gives ideas for children to explore and use **-er** and **-est** endings in different contexts. By the end of this unit, the children will be able to make distinctive comparisons and use these words effectively. Some of these words are repeated from Unit 2.

Curriculum focus:

Spoken language
- use relevant strategies to build their vocabulary

Reading comprehension
- discussing word meanings, linking new meanings to those already known

Spelling
- suffixes using **-er** and **-est**

1 Meet the words

Children watch a physical example of how the comparative suffixes work.

- Choose three different-sized children and stand them at the front of the class.
- Explain to the children that adding a suffix makes the comparison clearer.
- Say: [*Tom*] *is* tall, [*Joe*] *is* tall**er** *but* [*Ola*] *is* tall**est**. (You could display the slide on the PowerPoint available online at My Rising Stars to consolidate).
- Demonstrate the comparisons (sensitively!) with *short* and *small* too.
- Explain to the children that, like the word *tall*, the word *long* can also be demonstrated by the class. It means to measure distance from end to end.
- Ask the children to come up with a comparison of *long, longer, longest*, e.g. [*Luca's*] *hair is* long, [*Jessica's*] *hair is* longer *but* [*Jamila's*] *hair is* longest.

2 Explore meaning

Next, the children use the focus words to make comparisons.

Activity 1: *Short, tall* or *small*?

- In groups of three, ask the children to use the words *short, tall* or *small* to make a comparison.
- They need to be ready to tell the class what their comparison is.

Activity 2: *Long, longer, longest*

Now they are going to explore the word *long*.

- In small groups, ask the children to sort through strips of paper/thread/pipe cleaners of different lengths.
- Ask them to use the focus words *long, longer* and *longest* to describe the strips. E.g. *This strip is* long, *this strip is* longer, *but this strip is the* longest!

Play with words

The children work in pairs to examine comparisons in more detail.

● Ask them to think of three things they can describe using the focus words (e.g. plants, chairs, buildings, dogs, etc). Encourage them to make comparisons between these things. If appropriate, they could place items in order of size so they can see the comparisons. Some of the children can share their examples with the class.
● Label and make displays of comparisons.
● Address any misconceptions.

 Deepen understanding

Explain that these suffixes can be used for other comparisons.

● Reread the story of *The Three Little Pigs* from Unit 4 (p79).
● Ask: *How we can compare the three houses the pigs built using what we know about suffixes?*
● Model an example: *If the house of straw was* strong, *then the house of sticks was* strong**er** *and the house of bricks was the* strong**est***. Are there other words we can use?*
● Ask: *If we use the word* weak, *how could we describe the Three Little Pigs' houses?*
● The children may say the house of straw was the *weak**est***, the house of sticks was *weak* and the house of bricks was the *strong**est***.

Act it out

The children could act out the story of *The Three Little Pigs* but this time offer narration using the new focus words and suffixes.

Words at home

Ask the children to find three things when they are at home or out and about, and make comparison sentences using the suffixes **-er** and **-est**. They can share them with parents/carers or siblings.

Can you describe a mythical creature?

In context, fiction: The Book of Beasts by E. Nesbit

Words in this unit
Focus words
gentle
loose
shifting
feeble
shining
writhed
snatched
appeared
sprawling
pursued

You will need:
- RS Vocabulary Year 1 Unit 18 PowerPoint (available online at My Rising Stars)
- Extract from *The Book of Beasts* (see page 83 and available online at My Rising Stars)
- Hall or large area
- Whiteboard
- Tablet/camera
- Sound buttons

In a nutshell
In Year 1, the children become more familiar with descriptive language in different texts. This unit uses an extract from *The Book of Beasts* to generate activities that develop understanding of vocabulary in context. By the end of this unit, the children will have an understanding of how to use some of the words in different ways by developing their imaginations.

Curriculum focus:
Spoken language
- children should develop a capacity to explain their understanding of books and other reading
- use relevant strategies to build their vocabulary

Reading comprehension
- learning to appreciate rhymes and poems
- checking that the text makes sense to them
- discussing word meanings, linking new meanings to those already known
- drawing on what they already know or on background information and vocabulary provided by the teacher

1 Meet the words

The children meet the words when they see the picture of the hippogriff and hear the extract from *The Book of Beasts*.

- Read the extract (with feeling!) to the children (p83).
- Write up (or display) the focus words and read them out.
- Reread the text, asking the children to listen carefully for the focus words.
- Remind them that it is often possible to work out the meaning of a word by understanding the other words in the sentence.
- Read the focus words again and ask the children to tell a talk partner what they think they mean; ask some of them to suggest what the words mean to the class. Write their definitions on the board.
- Look at (display) the true definitions (see PowerPoint or Glossary online at My Rising Stars).
- Address any misconceptions.

2 Explore meaning

The children show the meaning of the words using their bodies.

- In a hall or large area, ask half the class to act out one of the focus words while the others watch. You may need to recap the meaning of the words (see 'Meet the words').
- Tell them the word quietly without the other group hearing.
- Ask the group watching to guess what the word is from the other group's actions, then swap over.
- *Shining* might be the trickiest to act out but see how inventive the children can be – they may try to act like the Sun or a star.

Play with words

The children listen to the sentences you read out one by one (use the PowerPoint to display/drag-and-drop – available online at My Rising Stars). They must choose the correct word to complete it. You may wish to recap meanings before you start.

Feeble or gentle?

o The dragon made a _____ roar and then gave up.
o The feather was _____ on my skin.
o The dragon was a _____ sight sprawled on the ground.
o The_____ king was kind to all the animals.

Loose or shifting?

o My tooth was _____ and it fell out.
o We were _____ the sand about.
o The _____ floorboards creaked as we walked on them.
o It was hard to walk on the bridge as it was _____ in the winds.

 Deepen understanding

● Ask the children, in pairs, to decide which of the focus words goes in each sentence. Make sure you display the focus words (either on the PowerPoint available online at My Rising Stars, on word cards or written).
● Ask one of the children to tell the class the correct focus word after each sentence.
  o Saheed was _____ on the sofa watching his favourite programme. (*sprawling*)
  o The dog _____ the cat, but the cat got away. (*pursued*)
  o "My tummy hurts," moaned Jo as she _____ in pain. (*writhed*)
  o The Sun _____ from behind a cloud. (*appeared*)
  o The Moon was_____ all night. (*shining*)
  o Elsa _____ the biscuit from the box. (*snatched*)

Word wise challenge

Ask some of the children to write their own story about a mythical beast. Challenge them to use some of the focus words. Children who find writing more challenging could tell their story on a tablet or recorder/sound button. They might then act out their stories and film them.

Words at home

Ask the children to retell the extract of the hippogriff and the dragon to a parent/carer or sibling. They should include as many of the focus words as they can remember.

19 What sound does it make?

Sounds from science investigations

In a nutshell

In Year 1, the children carry out simple tests and investigations. This unit offers activity ideas to make observations and have fun with vocabulary. By the end of this unit, the children will be able to identify and distinguish different sounds they hear and relate them to the world around them.

Curriculum focus:

Spoken language
- use relevant strategies to build their vocabulary

Reading comprehension
- discussing word meanings, linking new meanings to those already known

Science curriculum
- observing closely, using simple equipment
- performing simple tests

1 Meet the words

The children meet the words when they carry out simple science investigations.

Activity 1: Making bubbles

You can use washing up liquid and water to create bubbles for the children to look at.

- Explain to the children that the focus words relate to sounds.
- In an outdoor space, explain that they are going to make bubbles and listen to the sounds they make.
- Some children can blow bubbles from the bottles while others make larger bubbles with different-sized string and straws.
- Thread the string through the straws, then dip into the bubble mixture in the bucket to make a larger bubble.
- What sounds can they hear? (E.g. *pop*, *plop*, *slurp*, *splat*, etc.) Discuss and make a list on the playground with chalk or on the whiteboard/flip chart when you return to the classroom.

Activity 2: Making an explosion

- Explain to the children that the focus words relate to sounds.
- You will need to do this experiment with the children gathered around at a safe distance.
- In an outdoor space, carry out the investigation while the children watch and listen. They tell a partner what they hear.
- Open the bottle of fizzy drink, roll the paper up and put it in the bottle, using it as a funnel.
- Put five to seven mints in the bottle and quickly stand back to watch.
- (Instead, you could use a large tablespoon of baking soda, 200ml of water with a little splash of washing-up liquid and 400ml of vinegar for the same effect. Pour the water, vinegar and washing up liquid into an empty 2-litre bottle, then add the baking soda for the explosion.)
- See if the children can hear these sounds: *hiss*, *crash*, *buzz*, *fizz*, *plop*, *snap*, *pop*, *bang*, *slurp*, *splat*! Discuss as a class and write a list of sounds heard on the board.

Explore meaning

Recap the words listed in 'Meet the words' and make actions to represent them.

- In the outdoor space again, ask the children to think about one of the words that they heard during their investigations.
- Ask them to create a movement to show the sound that word made, e.g. a quick movement with their hands for *fizz* or slumping over for *plop*.
- Go through all the words and create movements.
- Half the class watch while the other half demonstrates a movement. Then swap.
- Pick out any really creative ideas for children to demonstrate to the class.

Play with words

Activity 1: Short or long?

Explore why some sounds are fairly short and others are longer.

- Make two columns on the whiteboard/flip chart.
- Ask the children which sounds they think are longer and which are shorter. Why do they think that? Ask: *What is it about the words that might make the sound short or long?*
- Say the short sounds very quickly: *buzz, fizz, hiss, pop, bang, snap.*
- Now say the longer sounds – *crash, plop, slurp, splat* – making them extra long.
- Underline the part of the word that is short or long (the vowel sound usually).

Activity 2: Fizz and plop

Now look at two sounds: *fizz* and *plop*.

- Ask the children to put their thumbs up if these things make a *fizz*.
  - a firework
  - a tree in the wind
  - a sparkling drink
  - a horse
  - a sparkler

- Ask the children to put their thumbs up if these things make a *plop*.
  - a stone dropping into a pond
  - a campfire
  - marshmallows being dropped into a mug of hot chocolate
  - the wind
  - a bee

Deepen understanding

Think of other objects/things that make the same sounds described by the focus words.

- The children choose four focus words, then draw and label four objects/things that make that sound.
- At the front of the class, go through each word and see how many things the class came up with that make that sound. Create a good list for each word. E.g. they could have firework – *fizz/bang*, doorbell or bee – *buzz*, twig – *snap*, pan dropped on the floor – *crash*, drinking a milkshake – *slurp*.

Words at home

The children find three things at home that make the sound of one of the focus words. They share what they have found with the class.

Who are the villains and heroes?

In context, fiction: Snow White and the Seven Dwarfs

Words in this unit

Focus words

boastful
rotten
stubborn
polite
jolly
trusting
tender
proud
fair
bashful

You will need:

- RS Vocabulary Year 1 Unit 20 PowerPoint (available online at My Rising Stars)
- A version of *Snow White and the Seven Dwarfs* (see pages 84–85 and PowerPoint available online at My Rising Stars)
- Whiteboard/flip chart
- Playground/hall

In a nutshell

In Year 1, the children listen to a variety of traditional tales and meet vocabulary that describes heroes and villains. This unit uses the story of *Snow White and the Seven Dwarfs* to explore different character traits. By the end of this unit, the children should know that a character can be described in very different ways to portray whether they are classed as a hero or a villain.

Curriculum focus:

Spoken language
- children should develop a capacity to explain their understanding of books and other reading
- use relevant strategies to build their vocabulary

Reading comprehension
- learning to appreciate rhymes and poems
- checking that the text makes sense to them
- becoming familiar with key stories, fairy stories and traditional tales, retelling them and considering their particular characteristics
- discussing word meanings, linking new meanings to those already known
- drawing on what they already know or on background information and vocabulary provided by the teacher

1 Meet the words

The children will meet the words by listening to the story.

- Read the story of *Snow White and the Seven Dwarfs* together (p84).
- *Who is/are the villains?* (stepmother, mirror) *Who are the heroes?* (Snow White, seven dwarfs, Prince Charming, huntsman).
- Reread the story. The children pick out the words that describe the characters (the focus words are in bold in the text).
- Write the words on the whiteboard/flip chart or display on the PowerPoint (available online at My Rising Stars).

2 Explore meaning

Activity 1: Definitions

Explain to the children that you are going to look at the focus words in more detail.

- Display the words and ask the children to discuss in pairs what each one means.
- Choose some partners to offer their definitions. Write them on the board.
- Display the true definitions for each word (see the PowerPoint available online at My Rising Stars).
- Compare with the children's attempts at definitions. *How are they different? Were they close?*
- Add any missing definitions and address misconceptions.

Definitions

boastful – someone who talks too proudly about what they have and do; **rotten** – someone who behaves in an unkind or mean way; **stubborn** – someone who will not change their mind or will not give up; **polite** – someone who has good manners and thinks about other people; **jolly** – someone who is happy and cheerful; **trusting** – someone who believes that other people are telling the truth; **tender** – someone who shows gentle and caring actions and feelings; **proud** – feeling pleased about something good that you have; you might also feel proud of someone else; **fair** – describes a person with light, blond or yellow hair. In the story of *Snow White*, however, it is used in an old-fashioned way, to mean beautiful; **bashful** – describes someone who is shy and easily embarrassed.

Activity 2: Heroes and villains

Play a game where you pretend to be the characters in the story (hot seating).

- First, discuss what makes a villain and what makes a hero.
- Choose a child and ask them to be a character of their choice from the story. They should act like the character and answer any questions that the children have for him/her.
- The class must guess if the character is a villain or a hero, and which character they are.
- Whoever guesses the character correctly can take a turn in the hot seat.
- Demonstrate how to play this game if the children haven't played before.

Play with words

Activity 1: Fill in the gaps

- Ask the children to listen to the sentences that you are going to read out and/or display (see the *Boastful or proud*? and *Tender or trusting*? slides on the PowerPoint available online at My Rising Stars).
- The children choose the correct word so that the sentence makes sense.

Now ask the children to discuss the following with a partner.

- o *Have you ever been* boastful? *What did you say?*
- o *Have you ever been* stubborn? *What did you do?*
- o *Have you ever been* polite? *How did it feel?*
- o *Have you ever been* bashful? *How did you behave?*

Ask the class if anyone would like to share their answers.

Activity 2: Act it out

Use a large space such as the playground or hall. Act out *boastful* and ask the children to have a go at being *boastful*. The children show each other how a *boastful* character would stand, walk, talk. Repeat for the other words. Draw the children's attention to how your body and movements change as you 'are' each word.

Deepen understanding

The children consolidate knowledge of the focus words by completing sentences.

- Display the sentences (see the PowerPoint available online at My Rising Stars). In pairs, the children decide which of the focus words complete each sentence.
- Ask one child to feed back after each sentence.

Word wise challenge

The children fold a piece of paper in half. On the top of the paper they write two sentences describing their character. Inside, they draw a picture of the character and write who it is. In pairs, the children read their sentences to one another. Can their partner guess which character they are describing? Open the paper to see if they are right. Discuss if the character is a hero or a villain.

Words at home

Ask the children to act out a character (using some of the focus words) at home, and ask the parents/carers or siblings to guess whether they are a villain or a hero.

Can we compare a fish and a duck?

Words relating to creatures

Words in this unit

Focus words
webbed feet
wings
bill
feathers
river
riverbank
tail
fins
gills
scales

You will need:

- RS Vocabulary Year 1 Unit 21 PowerPoint (available online at My Rising Stars)
- RS Vocabulary Year 1 Unit 21 'Can we compare a fish and a duck?' worksheets (available online at My Rising Stars)
- Four or five large pieces of paper
- Four or five felt tips
- Playground/hall
- Suggested stories:
  o *The Rainbow Fish* by Marcus Pfister
  o *The Ugly Duckling* by Hans Christian Andersen

In a nutshell

In Year 1, the children look at common animals and make simple comparisons. This unit offers a range of ideas for the children to learn the common features of a duck and a fish, and discover where they live. By the end of the unit, the children will be able to compare the two commonly found animals.

> ### Curriculum focus:
>
> **Spoken language**
> - use relevant strategies to build their vocabulary
>
> **Reading comprehension**
> - discussing word meanings, linking new meanings to those already known
>
> **Science curriculum**
> - describe and compare the structure of a variety of common animals (fish, birds)

1 Meet the words

The children look at the photos of the *river* and *riverbank* and the labelled diagrams of a duck and a fish (see the PowerPoint online at My Rising Stars).

- What can the children see in the photo with the ducks? Explain that *riverbank* means the land on the edge of a *river*.
- What do they see in the photo of the fish? Explain that the fish are swimming in the *river*, which is the water flowing between two *riverbanks*.
- Show them the two labelled diagrams, with the labels in the correct places, and explain that you are going to look at the different parts of the duck and fish.
- Choose a different child to tell you what each label says.
- Go through each of the focus words – *tail, fins, gills, webbed feet, wings, bill, scales, feathers* – and point them out on the pictures.

2 Explore meaning

Once the children have learned the words, look at what the parts of the animal do.

- Start with the duck – *webbed feet, wings, feathers*.
- Ask the children to suggest what webbed feet do. *How do they help the ducks?* If the children can't suggest answers, explain that webbed feet help the ducks swim easily through the water.
- Ask why ducks have wings. (These help them to move in the air and fly to different places for food.)
- Ask for suggestions about what the bill does. (It helps them sift through mud and water at the edge of the riverbank to find seeds, bugs and other food, while letting the water and the mud slip away.)
- Ask why ducks have feathers. (They help the duck to fly and keep warm and dry – they repel the water and make them waterproof).
- Now look at the fish – *tail, fins, gills, scales*.
- Ask the children to suggest what the tail and fins do. (They help fish to swim.)
- *What do gills do?* (Gills take oxygen out of the water to help them breathe, and let water carry away carbon dioxide, which they don't need. Fish force water through their gills, where it flows past lots of tiny blood vessels.)
- *What are the scales on a fish for?* (To protect the fish because they are quite hard, but they also show what kind of fish they are.)

Play with words

Activity 1: Spot the differences

Now compare the duck and the fish.

- The children work in groups around the classroom to find three differences between the duck and the fish. They can use the photos and labelled pictures to help them.
- Give each group a large piece of paper and a felt tip, and ask a confident writer in each group to act as scribe.
- Give them 15 minutes to discuss their answers and write them down.
- Let the children choose how they want to record their discussions. They should select one child to show their findings to the rest of the class.

Activity 2: Act it out

Ask the children to act out moving like a duck or a fish using the different body parts they have been learning about.

 Deepen understanding

The children consolidate learning by labelling diagrams of the duck and the fish with the focus words.

- Give the children the 'Can we compare a fish and a duck?' worksheets (available online at My Rising Stars), and model filling in one of the labels. They should do the rest themselves.
- Once finished, the children write underneath each picture where it can be found (*river* or *riverbank*).

Word wise challenge

You could read *The Rainbow Fish* and *The Ugly Duckling* to the children, and then ask them what physical features were significant in each story. The Rainbow Fish gave away her scales and The Ugly Duckling's feathers changed.

Words at home

Ask the children to look up (on the computer/tablet or in a book) another animal that has similar features to either a duck or a fish.

22 Which words describe a caterpillar?

In context, poetry: Caterpillars by Brod Bagert

Words in this unit

Focus words
sting
overnight
creepy
nasty
prickly
fuzz
squish
dewdrops
unsuspecting
disguise
living

You will need:
- RS Vocabulary Year 1 Unit 22 PowerPoint (available online at My Rising Stars)
- The poem *Caterpillars* by Brod Bagert (see page 86 and PowerPoint available online at My Rising Stars)
- Whiteboard/flip chart

In a nutshell

Children in Year 1 begin to look in more detail at poetry and making inferences. This unit uses a lively poem about caterpillars to develop vocabulary. By the end of the unit, the children will have acquired new descriptive words that they can use in their spoken and written language.

Curriculum focus:

Spoken language
- children should develop a capacity to explain their understanding of books and other reading
- use relevant strategies to build their vocabulary

Reading comprehension
- learning to appreciate rhymes and poems
- checking that the text makes sense to them
- discussing word meanings, linking new meanings to those already known
- drawing on what they already know or on background information and vocabulary provided by the teacher

Science curriculum
- identify and name common animals (caterpillar)

1 Meet the words

The children meet the words when you read the class the poem, *Caterpillars*.

- Read the poem to the class (p86).
- Write up the focus words and read them out.
- Reread the poem but ask the children to listen carefully, reminding them that it is often possible to work out the meaning of a word by understanding the other words in the sentence.
- Read the focus words again and ask the children to tell a talk partner what they mean.
- Ask some of the children to give their definitions.
- Write down as many of their definitions as possible and address any misconceptions.

Definitions
sting – a prick or a wound; **overnight** – throughout the night: taking a whole night; **creepy** – something that makes you feel icky and maybe even scared; **nasty** – very bad or unpleasant; **prickly** – describes something sharp, rough and pointy; **fuzz** – fluffy, soft hairs; **squish** – to crush or squash something, which makes a splashing sound; **dewdrops** – a drop of water, usually on grass; **unsuspecting** – when someone or something doesn't know that something is happening; **disguise** – when you try to look like someone/something else; **living** – alive now.

2 Explore meaning

Explain to the children that you are going to think about what the poem means.

- Reread the poem and ask the children what the poet thinks about caterpillars.
- Ask: *Can you tell me any words in the poem that gives us a clue as to how the poet feels about caterpillars?* (*Nasty, creepy, prickly.*)

- Ask the children to tell a partner which word lets us know that the living creatures didn't know what was happening. (*Unsuspecting*)
- Children ask their partner why the poet says that the caterpillars were in *disguise*. (Because they turn into butterflies.)

3 Play with words

Activity 1: Come to life!

Explain that you want to make the poem come to life.

- Ask the children to think of an action they could do for each of the focus words, then choose different children to suggest an action for each word.
- If they need help, you could suggest an action or demonstrate one, e.g. *overnight* could be a semi-circular arm movement.
- The actions should be performed when all the children are sitting on the carpet; they should be simple and only use the upper body.
- Reread the poem, doing all of the children's actions.
- Repeat with the children copying the actions.

Activity 2: Living or not?

Explain to the children that you want to think about what is *living* and what isn't.

- Remind the children of the meaning of *living* – something that is alive, rather than an object or a thing.
- Say some examples. If they are alive, the children should say *'living'*!
  - stone
  - a cat
  - a child
  - sand
  - plants
  - a snail
  - a pencil

4 Deepen understanding

Explain to the children that you would like them to answer 'yes' or 'no' to the questions below.

- Read the questions to them. Ask them to put their thumbs up if the answer is 'yes' and to put their thumbs down if the answer is 'no'.
  - *Is the dark lane* creepy?
  - *Can you* squish *a stone?*
  - *Is an apple* prickly?
  - *Is a* sting *painful?*
  - *Is a bus a living thing?*
  - *Do you find* fuzz *on a pencil?*
  - *If you are surprised have, you been* unsuspecting?

Words at home

Give the children a copy of the poem to take home. Ask them to reread the poem with their parents/carers or siblings and to teach them all the actions for the focus words.

23 What shall we choose in the playground?

Different movement words to describe a children's playground

Words in this unit

Focus words
wobbling
curling
scooting
slipping
padding
gripping
dangling
slamming
sagging
shoving

You will need:
- RS Vocabulary Year 1 Unit 23 PowerPoint (available online at My Rising Stars)
- String
- Focus words printed out
- Pegs
- A4 paper

In a nutshell

In Year 1, the children will be developing their understanding of action words. This unit offers teachers a range of ideas to enable the children to explore different words describing movement in a children's playground. By the end of this unit, the children will be able to describe different ways of moving and apply the words to different contexts.

> ### Curriculum focus:
>
> **Spoken language**
> - use relevant strategies to build their vocabulary
>
> **Reading comprehension**
> - discussing word meanings, linking new meanings to those already known

1 Meet the words

The children will meet the words by looking at the picture of the children's playground.

- Ask the children to talk to a partner about all the activities they can do at a children's playground.
- Introduce the focus words.
- Ask them what is the same about all the words. (They all end with -**ing**, which makes you think they are happening words.)
- Make a list of all the activities that would fit with those words in a playground. Below are some suggestions – the children may come up with their own ideas.
  - *wobbling* – on a balance frame
  - *curling* – on the circle swings
  - *scooting* – around a turning table
  - *slipping* – down a tube slide
  - *padding* – across a bridge
  - *gripping* – a rope swing
  - *dangling* – from a climbing ladder
  - *slamming* – the zip wire at the end
  - *sagging* – on a large rope swing
  - *shoving* – a swing

2 Explore meaning

Explain to the children that you are going to make a movement line.

- Hang a piece of string across the classroom.
- Write each focus word on a piece of card or print out the focus words (available online at My Rising Stars).
- Ask the children to think about the amount of movement each word makes.
- Explain that some of the words are large, quick movements, like *scooting*, and some are small and slow, like *padding*.
- Explain that you want to order the words from large and quick to small and slow.
- Say each word and ask the children to suggest where it should go on the line.
- Ask one of the children to peg up the words.
- The class can show whether they agree with the placement with a simple thumb up or down.
- The words can be moved around until everyone agrees with the order.

3 Play with words

Explain to the children that you would like them to think about other times you could use these words.

- Demonstrate how to fold a sheet of A4 into four quarters.
- Ask the children to draw four other things or places where they may use some of the focus words.
- Encourage them to share some of their ideas with the class.
- E.g. the jelly might have been seen *wobbling* on the plate, the taxi driver could have been *slamming* on the brakes when driving, or Grandpa may have been seen *padding* across the floor in his slippers!

4 Deepen understanding

Explain to the children that you would like them to think about how some focus words best suit how they would feel in certain scenarios.

- Ask the children: *How might you be feeling if:*
  - *You were* dangling *over a volcano of fire?*
  - *You were* gripping *tightly to the winning ticket at the fair?*
  - *You felt like* sagging *to the floor?*
  - *You were* curling *up under a blanket?*
  - *Someone was* slamming *into you in the playground?*
  - *You were* wobbling *on a skateboard, going very fast?*
  - *You were* scooting *on a bike?*
  - *You were* shoving *a very large trolley at the supermarket?*

Word wise challenge

Ask the children to make a list of any other doing words we could use to describe activities in a children's playground.

Words at home

Ask the children to notice which words describe their movements on different activities next time they go to a children's playground. Which focus words could they use?

In context, fiction: Sleeping Beauty

In a nutshell

In Year 1, the children will be listening to a variety of traditional tales and looking at the words and phrases relating to those tales. This unit offers teachers a range of ideas to enable the children to develop an understanding of how the words are used. By the end of this unit, the children will be able to use the focus words and phrases to develop their own traditional tales.

> ## Curriculum focus:
>
> **Spoken language**
> - children should develop a capacity to explain their understanding of books and other reading
> - use relevant strategies to build their vocabulary
>
> **Reading comprehension**
> - learning to appreciate rhymes and poems
> - checking that the text makes sense to them
> - discussing word meanings, linking new meanings to those already known
> - recognising and joining in with predictable phrases
> - becoming familiar with key stories, fairy stories and traditional tales, retelling them and considering their particular characteristics
> - drawing on what they already know or on background information and vocabulary provided by the teacher

1 Meet the words

The children will meet the words by listening to *The story of Sleeping Beauty*.

- Write up/display the focus words and phrases and read them to the children.
- Read the text (p87) and ask the children to listen carefully, reminding them that often it is possible to work out the meaning of a word by understanding the other words in the sentence.
- Read the focus words again and ask the children to tell a talk partner what each one means.
- Ask: *What clues tell us this is a traditional tale?* (Phrases such as *Once upon a time* and *happily ever after*, and words that relate to magic and enchantment.)
- Some of the children can suggest what the words mean.
- Write down as many of their definitions as possible, addressing misconceptions.
- Briefly sing/say the *Sleeping Beauty* song (see PowerPoint online at My Rising Stars), picking out the two focus words.

2 Explore meaning

Explain that you would like the children to retell the story using the language of traditional tales.

- Reread *The story of Sleeping Beauty*.
- Reread all the focus words and phrases within the text.
- The children work in groups of no more than four to retell the story in their own way, but including the focus words and phrases.
- Record their stories on a camera/tablet and watch them as a class.
- Ask the children not to speak but to put their thumb up when they recognise a focus word or phrase.

Play with words

Explain that you are going to look at a different form of the story, which is expressed as a poem or a song (see the PowerPoint available online at My Rising Stars).

- Teach the children the *Sleeping Beauty* song with actions – each verse is sung in a circle.
  - Verse 2: Sing/say while going round in a circle and putting hands together up high for the tower.
  - Verse 3: Sing/say while going round in a circle and waving a hand for a wand.
  - Verse 4: Sing/say while going round in a circle and shutting eyes and putting heads on one side with hands underneath to show sleep.
  - Verse 5: Sing/say while going round in a circle and twisting hands up to show the forest growing.
  - Verse 6: Sing/say while going round in a circle and doing a riding motion for the prince.
  - Verse 7: Sing/say while going round in a circle and making a cutting motion through the air with an imaginary sword.
  - Verse 8: Sing/say while going round in a circle and taking the imaginary hand and kissing the princess.
  - Verse 9: Sing/say while going round in a circle and clapping at the end.
- Ask if there any words repeated in the story and the song (*gallant* and *evil*).
- Ask:
  - *Which verse is the* Once upon a time *part in?*
  - *Which verse tells you they were all forgotten?* (The forest grew around)
  - *Which word means the same as the fairy giving Sleeping Beauty a bad wish?* (spell)
  - *How do you know the prince was brave?*
  - *Which verse tells us they lived* happily ever after?

 ## Deepen understanding

Explain that you would like the children to create their own traditional tale using the focus words and phrases.

- Display the focus words and phrases and reread them all.
- Provide dressing-up equipment.
- Ask the children to create their own tale/story in small groups using as many of the focus words and phrases as possible. However, tell them the story can develop in any way they like.
- If they would like to record their stories, they could use a camera or tablet.

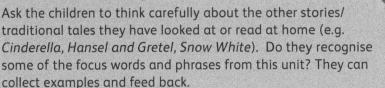

Word wise challenge

Ask the children to think carefully about the other stories/ traditional tales they have looked at or read at home (e.g. *Cinderella, Hansel and Gretel, Snow White*). Do they recognise some of the focus words and phrases from this unit? They can collect examples and feed back.

Words at home

Ask the children to retell the story at home to a parent/carer or sibling. They should make sure to include the focus words and phrases.

25 How many ways can you walk?

Words associated with movement

Words in this unit

Focus words
trot
shuffle
waddle
glide
dash
dodge
scamper
stumble
trudge
amble

You will need:

- RS Vocabulary Year 2 Unit 25 PowerPoint (available online at My Rising Stars)
- Playground/hall
- Word cards cut up, per group
- Two hoops from the PE cupboard
- 'Fast' and 'slow' cards cut up (available online at My Rising Stars)
- A set of focus word cards for each child to take home

In a nutshell

In Year 2, the children develop their knowledge of descriptive words. This unit provides activities that explore words to describe different ways of moving. By the end of the unit, the children will have acquired new language to describe movement, as well as understand the sometimes subtle differences between the words.

> ### Curriculum focus:
>
> **Spoken language**
> - the quality and variety of language that children hear and speak are vital for developing their vocabulary and grammar and their understanding for reading and writing
> - use relevant strategies to build their vocabulary
>
> **Reading comprehension**
> - discussing word meanings, linking new meanings to those already known
> - drawing on what they already know or on background information and vocabulary provided by the teacher

1 Meet the words

In this activity, the children become acquainted with the focus words and their definitions by acting them out and discussing them as a group.

- In the playground or hall, ask the children to find a space with enough room to move around freely.
- Read out each word and ask the children to demonstrate how they would walk in the style of that word.
- Take each word in turn, starting with *trot* (e.g. *trot* like a horse).
- Explain the definition of that word – to walk quickly, lifting legs up. Either display the words and their definitions in the hall (see PowerPoint online at My Rising Stars) or do it orally.
- After reading each definition, you may need to demonstrate and have the class copy you. Some of the words will be more well known than others.
- If any of the children know the movement, ask the class to copy them instead.
- Address any misconceptions and discuss the different words and their meanings.

2 Explore meaning

In this activity, the children sort the words into two groups – fast and slow – and then discuss the reasons for their choices.

- This could be a class or small-group activity. Time the children (or count to ten) so that they complete the task in a competitive spirit in their groups.
- Arrange two hula hoops on the carpet; inside one put the word 'fast' and in the other put the word 'slow'.
- Ask the children to sort each word card into the hoop they think it should go in. Listen to their discussion as they do so, and the vocabulary they use.
- When they have sorted all the words, pick a child to choose a word and explain why they put it into the 'fast' hoop.
- Ask a different child why they put their word into the 'slow' hoop.
- Continue with as many more words as necessary.

- Discuss whether all the groups/individuals agree and address any misconceptions.
- Did any groups think that a word could go into both groups? (Possibly *glide* because one can glide quickly or slowly, although generally it's a quicker motion.)

 ## 3 Play with words

Activity 1: Animal movements

The children use the focus words to explore how different animals move.

- In the playground or hall, ask the children to find a space so that they can move freely.
- You will need these words: *trot, waddle, glide* and *scamper*. Display them in the hall or put the word cards (available online at My Rising Stars) on the wall so that they are easily seen.
- Explain that the words not only describe ways that *we* might move but they can also be used to describe the way that animals move. In fact, some of the words are more associated with animals than with humans.
- Display the slides with the animal images (see PowerPoint available online at My Rising Stars). Tell the children that these words link to animals.
    - *waddle*: penguin, goose, duck
    - *trot*: horse, zebra, dog
    - *glide*: swan, eagle, hawk, seagull
    - *scamper*: mouse, puppy, kitten
- Ask the children to show you how to *waddle* like a penguin, *trot* like a horse, *glide* like an eagle or *scamper* like a mouse.
- Play a game where the children do an impression of an animal and the others, by looking at the *movement* (don't allow them to just act being the animal), guess what animal they are.
- You might also display an image of an animal and ask the children to make its movement, in order to consolidate knowledge of the vocabulary learned so far.

Activity 2: Act it out

- In this activity, offer children some scenarios. They must think and then tell you (or act out) what movement they would make, and whether it's a fast or slow one. E.g. skating on an ice rink (*gliding*); walking through the snow (*trudging*); having a walk on a Sunday with their family (*ambling*); having a snowball fight (*dodging, scampering, dashing*); waking up late for school (*dashing*).
- Afterwards, the children take the role of teacher and think up scenarios to lead the activity.

 ## 4 Deepen understanding

Explain to the children that they may use different forms of movement at different times.

- In pairs, ask the children to think about what choices they would make and feed back to the class.
- Would they:
    - dash *or* shuffle *away from a wasp?*
    - stumble *in mud or* scamper *through the long grass?*
    - glide *along in a boat or* trot *on a horse?*
    - dash *to the finish or* amble *along in a race?*
- After each question, discuss with the children why they have chosen that word.
- Allow the children to come up with some scenarios in pairs and pose the questions to the rest of the class for discussion.

> **Words at home**
>
> The children take a set of the focus words home. They must make the movement and ask their parents/carers or siblings to guess which one they are acting out. They can then discuss the definitions together. The children can feed back to the rest of the class how well their family guessed, which ones they got wrong, and why.

In context, poetry: The Dentist and the Crocodile by Roald Dahl

Words in this unit

Focus words

despair
require
repair
quivered
quaked
fearsome
probe
shook
harmless
cunning

You will need

- RS Vocabulary Year 2 Unit 26 PowerPoint (available online at My Rising Stars)
- The poem *The Dentist and the Crocodile* by Roald Dahl (see page 88 and PowerPoint available online at My Rising Stars)
- Whiteboard/flip chart/working wall

In a nutshell

In Year 2, the children listen to a variety of texts and infer what words mean in context. This unit provides a range of activity ideas to develop the ability to understand how words can be used effectively to create an impression. By the end of this unit, the children will have acquired new language from the poem and will be able to use it in different contexts.

Curriculum focus:

Spoken language
- children should develop a capacity to explain their understanding of books and other reading
- use relevant strategies to build their vocabulary

Reading comprehension
- checking that the text makes sense to them
- discussing word meanings, linking new meanings to those already known
- drawing on what they already know or on background information and vocabulary provided by the teacher
- making inferences on the basis of what has been said and done

1 Meet the words

Read the funny poem *The Dentist and the Crocodile* together (p88). Discuss with the children their reactions and what they think it's about.

- Write up or display the focus words (available online at My Rising Stars) and read them out.
- Reread the poem and ask the children to listen carefully for the focus words, reminding them that it is often possible to work out the meaning of a word by understanding the other words in the sentence.
- Read the focus words again and ask the children to tell a talk partner what they think each one means.
- Some of the children can suggest what the words mean and write their definitions on a working wall/whiteboard.
- Display the correct definitions (available online at My Rising Stars). Compare them to the class suggestions. How close were they? Address any misconceptions.

2 Explore meaning

Activity 1: Word detectives

- To understand the meaning of the words further, ask the children to make inferences from their knowledge of the poem. Explain that you want them to be detectives and look for evidence in the text to answer some questions.
- First, the children answer 'yes' or 'no' as a class. If the answer is 'yes', then they must put their thumb up; if the answer is 'no', then they must put their thumb down.
- Once they have answered 'yes' or 'no', it's important that the children explore the question 'why?' and answer as far as possible using evidence from the poem.
  - *Do you think the dentist is having fun? Why?*
  - *Do you think the crocodile is clever? Why?*
  - *Does the lady think the crocodile is scary? Why?*
  - *Did the dentist choose the longest probe? Why?*

Activity 2: Act it out

- The children should imagine they are the dentist and you are the crocodile coming to have your teeth looked at. Ask them to stand up and show, using their bodies and faces, that they are very scared. Read the poem again and ask the children to act out the role of dentist.

3 Play with words

Comparing words

Explain to the children that you would like to compare some of the words.

- Reread the poem and recap the meaning of the words *cunning*, *harmless*, *repair* and *require* (see the definitions available online at My Rising Stars).
- Display the cloze sentences (see the *Cunning or harmless?* and *Repair or require?* slides on the PowerPoint online at My Rising Stars). In pairs, ask the children to discuss which word should fill in the blank.
- Choose a child to complete each sentence and ask the class if they agree. (If using the PowerPoint display, you can drag and drop in the correct word.)

4 Deepen understanding

The following activity acts as a great opportunity to consolidate knowledge and make observations for assessment purposes.

- Say: *If I say something that is* fearsome *say:* fearsome. *If not, say:* nothing.
  - a teddy bear
  - a snarling tiger
  - a massive spider's web
  - a plate of rice
  - a pit of snakes
  - a pile of presents
- Then encourage the children to take the role of the teacher and create phrases to test their peers' knowledge. You can do this with some of the other focus words too.

Word wise challenge

Display the focus words on a whiteboard/flip chart. Ask the children to write their own example of a scary encounter in a familiar setting (e.g. a snake going to the doctor, a shark going for a swimming lesson), including as many of the focus words as possible.

Words at home

The children choose three focus words and think of three sentences that make sense using those words in. E.g. *Our dog is* harmless *because he is gentle*; *My cat is* cunning *because she creeps up on the birds*; *My sister* requires *a haircut because her hair is too long*. Each sentence should use 'because' to support and explain the answer.

27 How do you eat your food?

Words to describe eating

Words in this unit

Focus words

nibble
guzzle
munch
chew
feast
gobble
scoff
chomp
peck
gnaw

You will need:

- RS Vocabulary Year 2 Unit 27 PowerPoint (available online at My Rising Stars)
- Ingredients and appropriate area to make a pizza (for ingredients and recipe see the PowerPoint online at My Rising Stars)
- Whiteboard/flip chart or working wall
- Two hoops
- Sets of cards with focus words on
- 'Polite' and 'messy' cards cut up (available online at My Rising Stars)

In a nutshell

In Year 2, the children undertake many practical activities in different parts of the curriculum which act as terrific opportunities to develop vocabulary. This unit uses making a pizza as a starting point to gain knowledge of interesting onomatopoeic language to describe eating.

Curriculum focus:

Spoken language

- the quality and variety of language that children hear and speak are vital for developing their vocabulary and grammar and their understanding for reading and writing
- use relevant strategies to build their vocabulary

Reading comprehension

- discussing word meanings, linking new meanings to those already known
- drawing on what they already know or on background information and vocabulary provided by the teacher

1 Meet the words

First, the children make a pizza, and then they think about words to describe how they eat it. This is a great opportunity to immerse the children in an engaging practical activity while having fun with language.

- Ask the children to make a pizza (the recipe is available on the PowerPoint online at My Rising Stars). They can choose their toppings from a selection. They can either take their pizza home and share it with their family or they can eat it at school.
- Wherever they eat it, urge the children (and whoever else is eating it with them) to think of as many words as they can to describe what they are doing. E.g. did they *chew*, *nibble* or *scoff* their pizza?
- Ask them to think of as many other words as they can that are related to eating.
- Once every child has eaten their pizza, make a list together on the working wall or whiteboard of all the words they thought of.
- Go through each suggested word and ask the child who thought of it (others can help too) to suggest a definition.
- If any of the focus words are missed off the list, add them in and address any misconceptions.
- Display the definitions on the PowerPoint (available online at My Rising Stars) and compare. Do the children agree with the definitions here? Are they surprised by any?

2 Explore meaning

Activity 1: Sort the words

Ask the children to sort the focus words into two groups – 'polite' and 'messy'.

- Give small groups a set of the focus words (available online at My Rising Stars).
- Place two hoops on the carpet, one with a card saying 'polite' on it and the other saying 'messy'.
- Ask the children to think about the meanings of each word in their groups and sort them into two piles by placing them in the correct hoop.
- When they have all finished, ask the children to explain their choices. There may be much discussion over some of the words as they could be either polite or messy.

Activity 2: Creating sentences

The children can explore meaning further using the focus words to create sentences about how animals eat by using the words *nibble*, *chew*, *peck* and *gnaw*.

- In talking partners, the children discuss which animal might eat as the word suggests. E.g. *A dog* gnaws *on a bone.*
- Once the children have thought of an animal, they contextualise it by putting it into a sentence, which they can tell the rest of the class. E.g. *My dog* gnawed *on a juicy bone in the garden for two hours.*
- Repeat for *nibble, peck* and *chew*. Extend this activity to include any of the other 'eating' words as appropriate for the class.
- Share the sentences with the rest of the class, and ask them to peer review. How might they improve it? What do they like about it? Do they use the word correctly in the sentence?

 ## Play with words

Activity 1: Which word?

In this activity, the children choose between two words to complete the sentences so that they make sense. Ask the children to say the correct word to fill in the blank.

- Recap the meanings of the words *guzzle* and *gnaw* using examples before you start the activity. You can read out the sentences and ask the children to complete them (see the slide on the PowerPoint online at My Rising Stars). Repeat with the words *peck* and *feast*.

Activity 2: Act it out

Ask the children to show how they would eat for each of the focus words, reminding them of the definition first. Ask them how they will 'act out' *feasting*. They may suggest looking very satisfied and sitting up like a king or queen eating politely at a banquet.

 ## Deepen understanding

Yes/no questions are a great way to check understanding and consolidate knowledge of vocabulary. This activity will make clear those children that understand the new language and those that need more exposure to the words.

- Read the questions below to the children. Ask them to call out the answer 'yes' or 'no' as a class. Discuss answers, and ask the children to explain their answers fully.

  - *Can you* nibble *jelly?*
  - *Would you* feast *at a party?*
  - *If you* peck *at food are you* gobbling?
  - *Can you* scoff *soup?*

  - *Should you* guzzle *at a polite party?*
  - *Can you* chew *a smoothie?*
  - *Can a dog* nibble *a bone?*

- It can be fun for the children to take the role of teacher and think of questions for the rest of the class. This allows you to observe the children and deal with any misconceptions. Whenever you need to, return to the display with the definitions of the words.

Words at home

Ask the children to think of three animals and describe the way they eat. They can use the focus words or find some new ones. The children should report their findings to the rest of the class, maybe showing a video or a picture to illustrate their point.

In context, fiction: Hansel and Gretel

In a nutshell

In Year 2, the children can revisit familiar tales and use them as a vehicle to improve literacy skills, including vocabulary. This unit offers a range of ideas to develop understanding and use words in the context of a story. By the end of the unit, the children will be able to explain what the words mean in context and use them in their own writing.

Curriculum focus:

Spoken language
- children should develop a capacity to explain their understanding of books and other reading
- use relevant strategies to build their vocabulary

Reading comprehension
- checking that the text makes sense to them
- becoming familiar with key stories, fairy stories and traditional tales, retelling them and considering their particular characteristics
- discussing word meanings, linking new meanings to those already known
- drawing on what they already know or on background information and vocabulary provided by the teacher
- making inferences on the basis of what has been said and done

 1 ## Meet the words

The children listen to the extract from *Hansel and Gretel* (p89) and suggest definitions for the focus words.

- Remind them that this is a story they probably already know and ask two volunteers to retell the story in their own words.
- Explain that this time they are listening to a more detailed extract, not the whole story.
- Write up or display the focus words (available online at My Rising Stars) and read them out.
- Read the extract and ask the children to listen carefully, reminding them that often it is possible to work out the meaning of a word by understanding the other words in the sentence.
- Read the focus words again and ask the children to tell a talk partner what they mean.
- Ask some of the children to suggest definitions and write down as many as possible.
- Address any misconceptions.

2 ## Explore meaning

Activity 1: How would you feel?

Explain to the children that they need to imagine how they would feel in different situations.

- Ask them to imagine their facial expressions or body language if they had been *abandoned*. They can use their bodies but not make any sounds – demonstrate yourself.

- Read the following sentences and repeat the activity.

  - *If you were following a winding path in the forest.*
  - *If you were beneath looming trees.*
  - *If you were in a creepy room.*
  - *If you suddenly heard a booming sound.*

  - *If you heard someone murmuring a secret.*
  - *If you had got lost in the supermarket.*
  - *If you ate a scrumptious cake.*
  - *If you are celebrating your birthday.*

Activity 2: Act it out

Explain that you are going to act out different parts of the story (from p89 and on the PowerPoint) using narration and dialogue, but you will miss out some of the focus words. The children then have to guess which focus word you were acting out by inferring from the other dialogue and narration.

3 Play with words

Activity 1: Compare the words

Explain that you would like the children to compare two of the focus words.

- Ask the children to say the correct word to fill in the blanks (see the *Abandoned or lost?* and *Celebrating or scrumptious?* slides on the PowerPoint online at My Rising Stars).
- Choose a child to complete each sentence.

Activity 2: Check understanding

Next, read out some statements. If the children think it is describing something that is *winding*, ask them to say '*winding*'; if straight, they should say 'straight'. (If necessary, recap the meaning of 'straight'.)

  - *a snake wrapped around a tree*
  - *a pencil*
  - *a river weaving through the rocks*
  - *a spider weaving its web through the branches of a tree*

  - *a ruler*
  - *a maze*
  - *a door*

4 Deepen understanding

Explain to the children that you would like them to decide whether they are going to answer 'yes' or 'no'.

- Read the questions below to the children.
- Tell them on this occasion they can call out as a class the answer 'yes' or 'no'.

  - *Can a quiet voice boom?*
  - *Is celebrating fun?*
  - *Is something ordinary incredible?*
  - *Can small things loom over you?*

  - *Is delicious food scrumptious?*
  - *If you can't find something, is it lost?*
  - *Is a winding path straight?*

Words at home

Give the childre the words *abandoned* and *scrumptious* and ask them to write as many synonyms as they can find for each one at home. Make a class display of all the synonyms. Some of the children could create sentences using their synonyms and read them out in class.

Words in this unit

Focus words
pea green
wrapped
plenty
elegant
willing
dined
slices
edge
fowl
charmingly

You will need:

- RS Vocabulary Year 2 Unit 29 PowerPoint (available online at My Rising Stars)
- *The Owl and the Pussy-cat* poem (see page 90 and PowerPoint available online at My Rising Stars)

In a nutshell

In Year 2, the children become more familiar with poetry and develop their ability to make inferences. This unit provides ideas to gain understanding of vocabulary within the context of a well-known poem. By the end of this unit, the children will have an understanding of descriptive words and synonyms, and will discover some words used in the past.

Curriculum focus:

Spoken language
- children should develop a capacity to explain their understanding of books and other reading
- use relevant strategies to build their vocabulary

Reading comprehension
- learning to appreciate rhymes and poems
- checking that the text makes sense to them
- discussing word meanings, linking new meanings to those already known
- drawing on what they already know or on background information and vocabulary provided by the teacher

1 Meet the words

The children meet the focus words within the context of the poem *The Owl and the Pussy-cat*.

- Read the poem to the children (p90) or listen to an audio version together (search online).
- Write up the focus words (or display the PowerPoint – available online at My Rising Stars) and read them out.
- Reread the poem and ask the children to listen carefully for the focus words, reminding them that often it is possible to work out the meaning of a word by understanding the other words around it in the sentence.
- Read the focus words again – the children tell a talk partner what they think they mean when looking at them in context; ask some partners to feed back the possible meanings.
- Look at the real definitions (available online at My Rising Stars) and compare. Were they close? Address any misconceptions.

2 Explore meaning

Explain that there are some other tricky words in this poem.

- Ask them what they think is *sliced* in the poem. Can they tell by reading on?
- Write down their suggestions but ask them to explain their reasons.
- Explain that quince is a fruit (a bit like an apple) and ask them what they think the owl and the pussy-cat *dined* on. What is mince?
- Write down their suggestions but ask them to explain their reasons.
- Explain that mince is usually beef that is cut up into very small pieces.
- Explain that there is also some vocabulary that is associated more with the past. Reread the part of the poem with the word 'tarried'.

O let us be married! Too long we have tarried:

- Discuss what the children think 'tarried' means (waited). *Are there any clues in the verse?*
- Ask them what they think a shilling is (an old coin) and if there is any other money mentioned that we have now (a five-pound note).
- Do they know what a runcible spoon is (a fork curved like a spoon)? You could search online for it together.
- You could search online and show pictures of the items above and discuss.

 Play with words

Look again at the focus words and explore other words that could replace them in the poem.

- Discuss what is *wrapped* in the poem (honey and plenty of money).
- Ask the children what other things can be *wrapped* (presents, parcels, etc.)
- What else could be *pea green*? (a pea, the sea, clothes)
- What else could be a *fowl*? (a chicken, a turkey, a goose)
- Make a list of their alternative words.

 Deepen understanding

Activity 1: Change the words

To consolidate learning, change words in the poem to alternative ones with the same meanings.

- Reread the parts of the poem with *elegant, charmingly, willing*, and *edge* in.
- Ask the children, in small groups, to think of a replacement for one of the four words. It must fit in with the poem, so it needs to be similar.
  "You *elegant* fowl! (stylish, graceful, beautiful)
  How *charmingly* sweet you sing! (beautifully, nicely, delightfully pleasantly)

  "Dear pig, are you *willing* to sell for one shilling
  Your ring? (ready to, happy to, wanting to)

  And hand in hand, on the *edge* of the sand (near the water, at the end)
- Write down the groups' suggestions and review as a class whether they work.
- Reread the whole poem with their alternative suggestions.

Activity 2: Act it out

Ask the children to get into groups and act out each verse of the poem, taking turns to perform. How do they show someone being *elegant*? Ask the children to do different actions *elegantly*: walk across the room, sit down, open the door, etc.

Words at home

Ask the children to learn the poem by heart at home and recite it to their parents/carers or siblings. They can talk to their listener about what the focus words mean.

What is the weasel after?

In context, poetry: The Weasel by Ted Hughes

Words in this unit

Focus words

whizzes
hobbles
dither
hither
butchery
wonder
merry
creature
belly
mazes

You will need:

- RS Vocabulary Year 2 Unit 30 PowerPoint (available online at My Rising Stars)
- The poem *The Weasel* by Ted Hughes (see page 91 and PowerPoint available online at My Rising Stars)
- RS Vocabulary Year 2 Unit 30 'What is the weasel after?' worksheet (available online at My Rising Stars)
- Online clip of a weasel moving

In a nutshell

In Year 2, the children listen to a variety of poems and look at vocabulary in context. This unit offers a range of ideas to enable the children to work out meaning through inference and suggestion. By the end of this unit, the children will discover new vocabulary within the context of a fun poem, and will apply it to design and make their own maze.

Curriculum focus:

Spoken language
- children should develop a capacity to explain their understanding of books and other reading
- use relevant strategies to build their vocabulary

Reading comprehension
- checking that the text makes sense to them
- learning to appreciate rhymes and poems
- discussing word meanings, linking new meanings to those already known
- drawing on what they already know or on background information and vocabulary provided by the teacher
- making inferences on the basis of what has been said and done

Art and design
- to use drawing to develop and share their ideas, experiences and imagination

---

1 Meet the words

The children will meet the words by listening to the poem called *The Weasel* and watching a clip of how a weasel moves – search online.

- Write up or display the focus words (see PowerPoint online at My Rising Stars) and read them out.
- Read the poem (p91) and ask the children to listen carefully, reminding them that often it is possible to work out the meaning of a word by understanding the other words in the sentence.
- Read the focus words again and ask the children to tell a talk partner what they mean.
- Some of the children can suggest definitions – write down as many of these as possible.
- Address any misconceptions.

2 Explore meaning

Explain to the children that they need to be detectives and look for clues in the poem.

- Reread the poem and explain that you want them to answer some questions (below).
- Choose one child to give the answer and another to explain why.
  - ○ *In the first two lines, what word tells us the weasel is moving very quickly?* (whizzes)
  - ○ Hobbles *tells us how someone/something is walking. What other words describe how we walk?* (E.g. 'amble', 'trudge'. Think of the words covered in Unit 25)
  - ○ *What do the words* hither *and* dither *tell us about the weasel?* (He doesn't know where he is going.)

o *In verse 3, 'BLOOD' is written in capital letters. What does this verse tell you about what the weasel wants to do?* (He wants to kill and eat other animals.)
o *Look at the last verse. Why are we lucky and mice are not?* (Mice are small so the weasel chases them, but we are too big.)

 ## 3 Play with words

Explain to the children that you would like them to design a *maze* for the weasel and the mouse.

- Display the simple *maze* slide first, followed by the more complex one (see PowerPoint available online at My Rising Stars).
- Ask the children to plan their own *maze*. Explain that they need to put the weasel at the beginning and the mouse at the end. Children can use a blank piece of paper, or some children may find the scaffold worksheet useful (available online at My Rising Stars).
- Then say: *Make sure there is a clear route for the weasel – plan it out. Make sure there are a lot of dead ends, too. Then copy it out and decorate your* maze.
- They should swap *mazes* with another child and ask them to complete the *maze* to see if the weasel gets to the mouse.

 ## 4 Deepen understanding

Explain to the children that you would like them to write their own poem.

- Ask the children to choose a different animal.
- They should use as many of the focus words as they can or come up with other words to describe their animal.
- They may want to spend some time looking at images or videos of the animal moving around, and some may need to be given an animal and a scaffold to work to.
- They can write whatever they like, and it can be a rhyming poem or not. This should be an open, creative activity that allows children to use vocabulary to describe an animal rather than be too distracted by rhyming or metre.
- The children should plan what they will write first, showing their plans to their peers or to you first.
- When finished, ask some of the children to read out their poems.

Words at home

Ask the children to observe how animals behave at home. Can they use any of the focus words to describe them? It could be a pet or squirrel, badger, bird – anything they can see. Ask them to share their finding in 'show and tell' or carpet time.

31 Which habitat?

Words associated with animals and habitats

You will need:
- RS Vocabulary Year 2 Unit 31 PowerPoint (available online at My Rising Stars)
- Whiteboard/flip chart
- Sugar paper
- Drawing paper

In a nutshell

In Year 2, the children learn about the different *habitats* that animals live in. Although a science objective, it's a fantastic opportunity to introduce the children to interesting vocabulary and link to literacy work. This unit compares the different *environments* and *habitats* that animals can be found in. By the end of the unit, the children can use the science words with confidence, understand their meaning, and explain where they would rather live.

Curriculum focus:

Spoken language
- the quality and variety of language that children hear and speak are vital for developing their vocabulary and grammar and their understanding for reading and writing
- use relevant strategies to build their vocabulary

Reading comprehension
- discussing word meanings, linking new meanings to those already known
- drawing on what they already know or on background information and vocabulary provided by the teacher

Science
- identify that most living things live in *habitats* to which they are suited and describe how different *habitats* provide for the basic needs of different kinds of animals and plants, and how they depend on each other
- identify and name a variety of plants and animals in their *habitats*
- describe how animals obtain their food from plants and other animals, using the idea of a simple *food chain*

1 Meet the words

The children meet the words by looking at pictures of the *ocean* and *woodland*, thinking about the animals that live there, and learning the focus words that apply to the pictures.

- Show the children each picture (see the PowerPoint available online at My Rising Stars) and ask them to think about what animals would live in each one. Make a list of the animals on the whiteboard/flip chart:
  Ocean: turtles, octopus, stingrays, jellyfish, sharks
  Woodland: deer, owls, mice, hedgehogs, squirrels
- Introduce all the focus words and explain that you are looking at different *habitats* where animals live.
- Go through each focus word to see if the children know what it means. Do some words apply to one picture more than another?
- Choose a child to give you a suggested meaning before looking at the definitions (available online at my Rising Stars).
- Address any misconceptions.

2 Explore meaning

Explain that you would like to compare the two different *habitats*.

- Ask the children what the differences are for animals living in the *woodland* and the *ocean*.
- If they are looking at an *ocean habitat*, they imagine they are a stingray; if a *woodland habitat*, they imagine they are a mouse.
- Ask them to work in small groups.
- Give each group a large piece of sugar paper divided down the middle.
- On one side, ask one child in the group to act as scribe and write good, positive things about that *habitat* and on the other side not so good or negative things.
- Give them 10 minutes and then bring the class together to feed back by group.
- Take a vote with hands up on which is better: to live in an *ocean* or *woodland habitat*.

3 Play with words

Activity 1: What do the words mean?

Explain to the children that they are going to write down the focus words.

- Display the focus words (see PowerPoint online at My Rising Stars).
- Ask the children to write a sentence in their own words to explain what each word means.
- At the end of the activity, volunteers read out a sentence each.

Activity 2: Act it out

Explain that *predators* move stealthily to catch their *prey*. Ask the children to act out how a *predator* and its *prey* might move, e.g. how a *predator stalks* its *prey*, chasing, pouncing and striking. Then ask them to think about being the *prey*, running, dodging, scurrying and hiding.

4 Deepen understanding

Explain to the children that you would like them to decide whether these statements are true or false.

- Read the statements below to the children.
- They show if they think they are true by putting a thumb up or false by putting a thumb down.
  - *A rabbit's* shelter *is a burrow.*
  - *A shark is a* prey.
  - *An owl lives in an* ocean habitat.
  - *Turtles live in an* ocean habitat.
  - *An owl and mouse are part of the same* food chain.
  - *A mouse is a* predator.
  - *A food chain is made of biscuits.*
  - *A fox is a* predator.
  - Prey *chases* predators.
  - *Can animals live in micro-habitats?*

Word wise challenge

Ask the children, in pairs, to revisit the desert picture (see the PowerPoint). Using the focus words, can they discuss, in pairs, some of the animals who might live in that habitat and how they would behave? You could prompt them if needed (i.e. camel, scorpion, lizard etc.). As a class, look at the picture and talk about what the children have noticed and how they have applied their focus words.

Words at home

Ask the children to think about where they live (town, village, city, etc.) and about the animals that live in their *habitat*. Give them some paper and see if they can draw and label their *habitat*. Encourage them to see how many focus words they can use.

Can you describe the landscape?

Words to describe geographical settings

Words in this unit

Focus words

beach
cliff
coast
forest
mountain
sea
ocean
river
valley
vegetation

You will need:

- RS Vocabulary Year 2 Unit 32 PowerPoint (available online at My Rising Stars)
- Focus words cut up
- Definition cards cut up (available online at My Rising Stars)
- A set of cards with the focus words and their definitions written together (available online at My Rising Stars)

In a nutshell

In Year 2, the children might learn geographical features within their wider curriculum work. This offers an engaging opportunity to look at the vocabulary of physical features in landscape. This unit offers a range of ideas to enable the children to clarify their understanding of geographical vocabulary. By the end of this unit, the children will be able to distinguish different and similar physical features and talk about their own environment.

Curriculum focus:

Spoken language
- the quality and variety of language that children hear and speak are vital for developing their vocabulary and grammar and their understanding for reading and writing
- use relevant strategies to build their vocabulary

Reading comprehension
- discussing word meanings, linking new meanings to those already known
- drawing on what they already know or on background information and vocabulary provided by the teacher

Geography
- use basic geographical vocabulary to refer to:
  - key physical features, including: *beach, cliff, coast, forest*, hill, *mountain, sea, ocean, river*, soil, *valley, vegetation*, season and weather

1 Meet the words

The children will meet the words by matching them with their definitions.

- Explain that you are looking at words relating to different physical features of the land. Some they may know and some not.
- Ask the children to work in small groups.
- Give each group a set of focus words and a set of their definitions, (see Focus word cards available online at My Rising Stars) and ask them to match the correct word with its definition.
- When they have completed the task, bring the class together and go through each word and match it with the correct definition.
- Display them on a board (available online at My Rising Stars).

Definitions

beach – a pebbly or sandy shore by the sea; **cliff** – a steep rock face, especially at the edge of the sea; **coast** – the part of the land adjoining or near the sea; **forest** – a large area covered chiefly with trees and undergrowth; **mountain** – a large natural elevation of the Earth's surface rising abruptly from the surrounding level; **sea** – an expanse of salt water; **ocean** – a very large sea; **river** – a large natural stream of water flowing in a channel to the sea, a lake or another river; **valley** – a low area of land between hills or mountains, typically with a river or stream flowing through it; **vegetation** – lots of plants living together.

2 Explore meaning

Explain to the children that you want them to match the definitions with a picture.

- Explain that you have a picture to match each focus word (see the Focus word cards available online at My Rising Stars).
- Give each group a set of pictures and a set of cards with the definitions and focus words together (available online at My Rising Stars).
- Ask the children to match them up in their groups.
- Bring the children back together as a class and decide which picture goes with which word. Display the pictures next to the words.

3 Play with words

Explain to the children that you want to look at the words in more detail.

- Ask them to look at the focus words carefully.
- Working in pairs, ask the children to tell their partner which ones are similar: *sea/ocean/river; coast/beach/cliff; vegetation/forest.*
- The children choose one of the groups of words and, still in pairs, think of an explanation for the main difference between them. E.g., a *river* is long and thin; the *sea* is big; and an *ocean* is enormous.
- Encourage them to share some of their explanations with the class.

4 Deepen understanding

Explain to the children that you would like them to decide whether these statements are true or false.

- Read the statements below to the children.
- They can show if they think they are true by putting a thumb up or false by putting a thumb down.
  - *A* valley *is a raised piece of ground.*
  - Vegetation *means where lots of plants are growing.*
  - *A* cliff *is flat.*
  - *You have to climb very high to get to the top of a* mountain.
  - *The* coast *is where the land meets the* sea.

Allow the children to play the teacher and create their own statements. They can read them to the class who put their thumb up or down, as appropriate.

Words at home

Ask the children to think about the physical features of where they live. They write a short description of their environment, using the focus words if possible. Tell the children they can use other similar words they know – like 'hill', 'flat', 'seaside' and 'wood' – to describe their area, e.g. *I live in a* valley *a long way from the* coast. *We are surrounded by hills and there is a little wood at the back of the house.*

---

33 How do we grow tomato plants?

In context, non-fiction: Life Cycles of Tomato Plants by Siobhan Skeffington

Words in this unit

Focus words

pests
harvest
protect
harmful
fertile
sown
seedlings
ripe
liquid
sub-tropical

You will need:

- RS Vocabulary Year 2 Unit 33 PowerPoint (available online at My Rising Stars)
- *Life Cycles of Tomato Plants* text (see page 92 and PowerPoint available online at My Rising Stars)
- A tomato plant (if possible, to show the class or to grow in the class)
- Ripe tomatoes of various sizes
- The book *Aliens Love Underpants* by Claire Freedman and Ben Cort
- Playground/hall
- School library
- Computers/tablets
- Paper
- RS Vocabulary Year 2 Unit 33 'How do we grow tomato plants?' worksheet (available online at My Rising Stars)

In a nutshell

In Year 2, the children will be learning about words relating to the life cycles of plants. This unit offers teachers a range of ideas to enable the children to explore how the tomato plant grows and develops. By the end of this unit, the children will be able to explain the life cycle independently and apply the focus words to other plants.

Curriculum focus:

Spoken language
- children should develop a capacity to explain their understanding of books and other reading
- use relevant strategies to build their vocabulary

Reading comprehension
- checking that the text makes sense to them
- discussing word meanings, linking new meanings to those already known
- drawing on what they already know or on background information and vocabulary provided by the teacher

Science
- observe and describe how seeds and bulbs grow into mature plants
- find out and describe how plants need water, light and a suitable temperature to grow and stay healthy

1 Meet the words

The children will meet the words by listening to the non-fiction text.

- Explain to the children that you would like to talk to them about tomato plants.
- Explain that you are going to read a short non-fiction text (p92), that will give them some information. You will also show them a plant and some tomatoes.
- When you have read the text, ask the children if there were any words they were unfamiliar with (probably *fertile* and *sub-tropical*).
- Explain *sub-tropical* using a globe to show where these regions are.
- Ask the children to volunteer the meaning of some of the focus words. Clarify any they are unsure of.

2 Explore meaning

Explain to the children that you are going to think about how plants grow.

- Take the children to a large area (playground/hall) to act out how a tomato plant grows.
- First, ask them to curl up small, like a seed.
- Pretend to pour water onto them, as you wander around the space. Tell the children what you are doing and ask them what they think will happen to the seed. They should start to grow a little more as the water is added.
- Soon, they will sprout leaves. The children should show this with their bodies and discuss what they are showing.
- Now, you can act as the hot sun shining. Again, explain to the children what you are doing. Ask the children to act out what will happen (they will grow more).
- Tell the children that, at this point, they are called *seedlings*.
- Next, they have to transplant themselves into a pot as they become bigger.

- They *ripen* both in the sunshine and with more water.
- Again, walk around the space, but this time offer them *liquid* food. They can make their hands into tomatoes as they grow more.
- Finally, once all the tomatoes have grown, they are *ripe* and ready for *harvest*.

3 Play with words

Explain that you want the children to think very carefully how they can show the information they know. (You could start by reading the book *Aliens Love Underpants* by Claire Freedman and Ben Cort to put this exercise into context.)

- The children look at the tomato plant and the tomatoes.
- In pairs, they explain to each other how it grows and what you need to do to make sure it survives. You could remind them to recap how they acted out the tomato plant growing in *Explore meaning*.
- Explain that you would like them to a draw a simple flow chart (template available online at My Rising Stars) of how a tomato grows. This is for an alien who has never been to Earth before, and you would like to give him a tomato plant.
- You need to include as much information in pictorial form with just focus words on the picture.
- Talk to the children about how to make their information very clear.
- Display their flow chart posters around the room.

4 Deepen understanding

Explain that you would like the children to decide whether they are going to answer 'yes' or 'no' to some statements.

- Tell them that, on this occasion, they can call out as a class, answering 'yes' or 'no' to the following.
  - *A pest* helps plants grow.
  - *Water is a* liquid.
  - *You* harvest *fruits and plants when they are ready to eat.*
  - *Something that is* harmful *is good for plants.*
  - Fertile *soil is good for growing plants.*

Word wise challenge

Ask the children to use their focus words to explain how another plant grows. They could research this in the school library or on a computer/tablet. Ask them to make a simple flow chart to show what happens.

Words at home

Ask the children to explain the life cycle of a tomato plant to their parents/carers or siblings. They should ensure they have used the focus words in their description. Can they look up online – or find out from their family – other plants and how they grow? The children can report back during carpet time.

In context, poetry: The Garden by Andrew Marvell

Words in this unit

Focus words

wondrous
luscious
crush
curious
vine
ensnared
fountain
mossy
casting
plumes

You will need:

- RS Vocabulary Year 2 Unit 34 PowerPoint (available online at My Rising Stars)
- The poem *The Garden* by Andrew Marvell (see page 94 and PowerPoint available online at My Rising Stars)
- Whiteboard/flip chart
- Focus words
- Pinboard/working wall
- Computers/tablets

In a nutshell

In Year 2, the children listen to a variety of poems and extend their vocabulary through different contexts. This unit uses the poem *The Garden* by Andrew Marvell to generate activities around inference and suggestion. By the end of the unit, the children will have acquired new language from the poem, found synonyms for the focus words, and written their own description of a garden.

Curriculum focus:

Spoken language
- children should develop a capacity to explain their understanding of books and other reading
- use relevant strategies to build their vocabulary

Reading comprehension
- checking that the text makes sense to them
- learning to appreciate rhymes and poems
- discussing word meanings, linking new meanings to those already known
- drawing on what they already know or on background information and vocabulary provided by the teacher
- making inferences on the basis of what has been said and done

Computing
- use technology purposefully to create, organise, store, manipulate and retrieve digital content

1 Meet the words

The children meet the words by listening to the poem *The Garden* by Andrew Marvell (p94) and suggesting definitions, using the context of the poem to help. They compare their definitions with those on the PowerPoint (available online at My Rising Stars) and discuss differences and similarities.

- Read the poem to the children and display it on the whiteboard.
- Write up/display the focus words and read them out.
- Reread the poem, asking the children to listen carefully for the focus words.
- Remind them that it is often possible to work out the meaning of a word by understanding the other words in the sentence.
- Read the focus words again and ask the children to tell a talk partner what they think each one means.
- Ask some of the children to suggest definitions, and write down as many as possible.
- Now compare them with the definitions on the PowerPoint. Were they close? Did any of the meanings surprise them? Address any misconceptions.

2 Explore meaning

In this activity, the children explore the meaning of the words further, within the context of the poem. They do this by answering a series of yes/no questions.

- Reread the poem and inform the children that you want them to answer some questions.

- Choose one child to give the answer, and another to explain why, using evidence from the poem where possible. Other children can help with this.
  - *In the first verse, the poet mentions five fruits; apples, nectarines, peaches, melons and what was the other one?* (grapes) *What clues give you the answer?*
  - *In the second verse, the poet refers to a bird. Can you say three words that show this?* (sits, sings, wings, flight and *plumes*)
  - *Why did you choose those words?*
- Encourage the children to think of their own question(s) about the poem. They can become the teacher and pose their question to the class, or the activity can take place in pairs/small groups.

 ## 3 Play with words

Synonyms

The children research the words online and find synonyms for them in order to create a pinboard display or working wall.

- Working in mixed-ability pairs on a computer/tablet, give the children a list of some of the focus words: *wondrous, luscious, crush, curious, ensnared* and *casting.*
- Ask them to type their words and 'synonym' into a search engine to find other words that mean the same thing. The children should write down two or three synonyms for each word.
- At the end of the session, the children talk through the words that they found and create a class pinboard/display with the words and their synonyms.
- Possible synonyms for the words: *wondrous* – amazing, astonishing, miraculous, striking, wonderful; *luscious* – appetising, delicious, succulent, yummy, heavenly; *crush* – mash, squash, squeeze, press; *curious* – inquisitive, analytical, inquiring, examining; *ensnared* – captured, imprisonment, held; *casting* – flinging, hurling, chucking.

 ## 4 Deepen understanding

Explain that you would like the children to think of using the focus words in different contexts.

- Ask them to tell a partner how they would feel if…?
  - *You were suddenly being* crushed.
  - *You were given a* luscious *pudding.*
  - *You were* curious *to know what was under your bed.*
  - *You were* ensnared *in a net in the forest.*
  - *You suddenly grew* plumes *on your arms.*
  - *You put your bare feet on a* mossy *log.*

Word wise challenge

Ask the children to think of descriptive words they could use to describe their own garden or a garden they have visited. Explain to the children that you would now like them to use some of the focus words, as well as their descriptive words, to write a description of their garden.

Words at home

Ask the children to think of as many different words as they can relating to gardens and plants. They can discuss the focus words and the poem with their parents/carer or siblings for inspiration. You could discuss some of these words together at carpet time.

35 Will you listen to our song about the Great Fire?

Words relating to musical composition

Words in this unit

Focus words
percussion
compose
perform
musician
tune
beat
volume
conductor
rhythm
accompany

You will need:

- RS Vocabulary Year 2 Unit 35 PowerPoint (available online at My Rising Stars)
- Musical instruments – a variety of percussion instruments: wooden blocks, drums, maracas, bells, tambourines
- Whiteboard/flip chart

In a nutshell

In this unit, the children learn about the Great Fire of London and create a piece of music. In doing so, they extend their vocabulary of musical words and terms. The work here can be used within a more extended topic on the Great Fire of London very effectively, or as a standalone lesson if the children have already covered the topic in a previous year group.

Curriculum focus:

Spoken language and reading comprehension
- the quality and variety of language that children hear and speak are vital for developing their vocabulary and grammar and their understanding for reading and writing
- drawing on what they already know or on background information and vocabulary provided by the teacher

Music
- use their voices expressively and creatively by singing songs and speaking chants and rhymes
- experiment with, create, select and combine sounds using the interrelated dimensions of music

History
- events beyond living memory that are significant nationally or globally (for example, the Great Fire of London)

1 Meet the words

The children meet the words when they listen to a short account of the Great Fire of London and sing the nursery rhyme *London's Burning*.

- Read the short description of the Great Fire of London (see PowerPoint online at My Rising Stars). Have the children heard of it before? What do they know? Discuss. What were the changes made after the fire to stop it from happening again? Write a list on the whiteboard.
- Next, sing *London's Burning* together (the verse is on the PowerPoint online at My Rising Stars). The children will probably be familiar with the *tune*.
- Say all of the focus words (see PowerPoint online at My Rising Stars) and display them. Ask the children what they think they will be asked to do (create music!).
- Looking at the focus words again, ask the children to think about what each word means and feed back. Some of the words will be quite familiar to children, others less so.
- Ask for volunteers to suggest what they mean.
- Display the words and their definitions and discuss them together. Are there any words that are new to the children? When have they come across them before (if they have)?

2 Explore meaning

Now it is the children's opportunity to be creative. If they have done the 'Meet the words' activity, it will be no surprise that they will be creating music. The children may have already guessed that they will be accompanying the *tune* with musical instruments.

- Divide the children into five groups. Each group chooses two *percussion* instruments. The others in the group clap their hands.
- Sing the song together again all the way through. First, see if the children can follow the *rhythm* with you just by clapping their hands.
- If they have an instrument, ask them to follow the same *beat* using the instrument (some may tap a drum with their fingers, others use a stick – allow them to be creative).
- Remind the children that they need to think about the *beat* and the *volume*. Will they change the *volume* as they play? Some might play loudly and the singing won't be heard!
- While one group is playing, the other children sing.
- Give the groups some time to work together and encourage them to use some of the focus words in their rehearsals. They could create different *beats* or use their instruments differently now.
- Some children might use the musical instruments to show what is happening in their verse.
- As you work with the children, use and emphasise the focus words. E.g. call the children *musicians*, and refer to yourself as the *conductor*. The children are singing the *tune* and clapping the *beat*. It is important that they hear the words used in context.

3 Play with words

Together, *perform* the song with instrumental accompaniment.

- You will take the role of *conductor* so that the different groups know when to begin.
- Divide the children into three groups: the first group play their instruments and the other two sing the song as a round. Swap around so all children get to play the instruments.
- Have a run through together first, before *performing* it to another class.
- You could also video the performance and show it back to your own class. Allow the children to review their own work. How could they improve? What did they like about it?

4 Deepen understanding

Next, the children *compose* their own accompaniment to a song of their choice and *perform* it to the rest of the class. Praise children when they use the focus words in their rehearsals.

- Each group chooses a song they know well and then *composes* a simple accompaniment to it using *percussion*.
- Ask questions. E.g. Can they work out the *rhythm* and the *beat*?
- What is the *tune*? Who will be singing and do they know the words? Would they like to *perform* it to the class?
- Could someone be the *conductor*? What will they do? How will they *compose* the accompaniment?
- What will the *volume* be at the beginning and will it change? Let the children in the group decide who is singing, who is playing and if they would like to *perform* to the class or not.
- Each group (whether they *perform* or not) should explain what they did to the rest of the class, ensuring that they use the focus words in their explanation.

Words at home

Ask parents/carers and siblings to listen to a performance of their child at home singing the song *London's Burning* and clapping along. The children can then explain what the focus words mean and what they have learned about the Great Fire of London. Urge the children to talk to their parents/carers and siblings about other songs they know about events in history (British or otherwise).

What is the myth of Demeter and Persephone?

In context, fiction: Persephone and the Pomegranate Seeds by Geraldine McCaughrean

36

Words in this unit

Focus words

meanwhile
wilted
myth
gazed
searched
disappeared
wept
despair
hopeless
stolen

You will need:

- RS Vocabulary Year 2 Unit 36 PowerPoint (available online at My Rising Stars)
- Background and extract from the Greek myth *Persephone and the Pomegranate Seeds* (see pages 95–96 and PowerPoint available online at My Rising Stars)
- Whiteboard/flip chart
- Small individual whiteboards/ marker pens/ wipes

In a nutshell

In Year 2, the children will be listening to a variety of traditional tales, including Greek *myths*, and looking at words that describe emotions. This unit offers teachers a range of ideas based around the *myth* of Demeter and Persephone, to enable the children to develop their ability to understand the words in context. By the end of this unit, the children will be able to answer questions relating to their understanding of the focus words and the text.

Curriculum focus:

Spoken language
- children should develop a capacity to explain their understanding of books and other reading
- use relevant strategies to build their vocabulary

Reading comprehension
- checking that the text makes sense to them
- becoming familiar with key stories, fairy stories and traditional tales, retelling them and considering their particular characteristics
- discussing word meanings, linking new meanings to those already known
- drawing on what they already know or on background information and vocabulary provided by the teacher

1 Meet the words

- Read the background and extract to the children (p95 – repeat, if needed, so that the children can become familiar with the names of the characters in the *myth*).
- Write up the focus words and read them out.
- Read the extract again and ask the children to listen carefully for the focus words.
- Remind them that it is often possible to work out the meaning of a word by understanding the other words in the sentence.
- Read the focus words again. The children should talk in pairs about what they think the words mean, given how they are used in the extract. Assign certain words to certain pairs if there are too many, or only focus on some of the words.
- Encourage the children to suggest what the words mean – write down as many of their definitions as possible.
- Look at the definitions provided in the PowerPoint and compare them. How close were the children's suggestions? Address any misconceptions.

2 Explore meaning

Vocabulary detectives

- Reread the background and extract and say you want them to answer some questions.
- Ask individual children to answer the questions.
    - *Why was Demeter searching for her daughter?* (It was time to go home; they had finished work as it was the end of the day.)
    - *What season had arrived because Demeter hadn't found Persephone?* (Autumn)
    - *How can you tell? What is the evidence?* (The leaves were going yellow and brown, the crops stopped growing and the flowers *wilted*.)

To extend the task, ask the children to create their own questions, in pairs, to ask the class.

Play with words

Activity 1: What's the missing word?

- Provide the children with their own whiteboard or chalk board (or paper if not possible).
- Read each sentence individually to the children (see the *What's the missing word?* slide on the PowerPoint online at My Rising Stars).
- Reread the first sentence. Ask them to write the correct focus word on their whiteboard. They hold them up when they have finished so that you can see and address any misconceptions.
- Repeat for the other sentences.
- There is an opportunity here to check the children's spelling and correct it; however, remember that the purpose of the activity is to ensure that the children understand the vocabulary and can see its use in context. The children can peer review work and help one another to answer correctly.

Activity 2: Vocabulary detectives

Explain that the children will work as detectives to answer questions and look for clues in the text.

- Read out the following questions, one by one. Choose one child to give the answer but another to explain why.
  - *How did Demeter feel when she sat by the river?* (In *despair*.)
  - *Can you give another word for* despair*?* (*hopeless*, unhappy, sad, depressed)
  - *Can you act the word* 'despair'*? How might Demeter look and move?*

Ask the children, in pairs, to think of three more questions about the text. They ask the pair next to them to work as detectives to find the answer and give evidence using the text. Pairs can feed back their questions and answers to the class at the end of the session.

 ## Deepen understanding

Together, check understanding of the vocabulary learned. The children answer a series of questions with 'yes' or 'no'. This enables them to have more exposure to the words used in context and deepens their understanding.

- Explain that, on this occasion, they can call out as a class when they answer 'yes' or 'no' to the following questions.
  - *Is it* hopeless *when you think nothing is going to get better?* (yes)
  - *Is a* gaze *a quick look?* (no)
  - *If you have something that is* stolen, *is it yours?* (no)
  - *Do plants bend down when they* wilt? (yes)
  - *Can you see something that has* disappeared? (no)

Words at home

At home, the children research Greek **myths**. *Where do they come from, and when? What were they used for and how important are they?* The children choose a *myth* and retell it during carpet time. Have a Greek *myth* story-telling session where the children can ask and answer questions about the myths told them by their classmates.

When Goldilocks went to the house of the bears,

Oh what did her blue eyes see?

A bowl that was **huge**,

A bowl that was **small**,

A bowl that was **tiny** and that's not all,

She counted them: one, two, three.

When Goldilocks went to the house of the bears,

Oh what did her two eyes see?

A chair that was **huge**,

A chair that was **small**,

A chair that was **tiny** and that's not all,

She counted them: one, two, three.

When Goldilocks went to the house of the bears,

Oh what did her two eyes see?

A bed that was **huge**,

A bed that was **small**,

A bed that was **tiny** and that's not all,

She counted them: one, two, three.

When Goldilocks ran from the house of
the bears,

Oh what did her two eyes see?

A bear that was **huge**,

A bear that was **small**,

A bear that was **tiny** and that's not all,

They growled at her: grrr, grrr, grrr!

Once upon a time there were three little pigs.

The first pig built a house made of straw, while the second pig built his house with sticks. They built their houses very quickly because they were lazy and wanted to sing and dance all day.

The third little pig wasn't lazy. He worked hard all day and built his house with bricks. The Big Bad Wolf saw the pigs and thought, "What juicy, tender meals they will make!" He chased the pigs and they ran and hid in their houses.

The Big Bad Wolf went to the house made of straw, where the first little pig was hiding. He said, "Let me in, let me in, little pig, or I'll huff and I'll puff and I'll blow your house in!"

"Not by the hair of my chinny chin chin," said the little pig. But of course the wolf did blow the house in. The first little pig ran to where the second pig lived, and hid.

The wolf then came to the house of sticks. "Let me in, let me in, little pig, or I'll huff and I'll puff and I'll blow your house in."

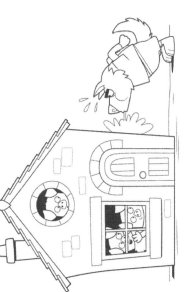

"Not by the hair of my chinny chin chin," said the little pig. But the wolf blew that house in, too. The first and second little pigs ran to the brick house to hide from the Big Bad Wolf.

Finally, the wolf went to the house of bricks. "Let me in, let me in," cried the wolf, "or I'll huff and I'll puff till I blow your house in."

"Not by the hair of my chinny chin chin," said the pigs. Well, the wolf huffed and puffed but he could not blow the brick house down.

The sly old wolf tried to get into the house down the chimney, but the third little pig had boiled a big pot of water and kept it at the bottom. The wolf fell into it and was burnt!

The other two pigs rebuilt their houses with bricks, and they all lived happily ever after.

Once upon a time there was a boy named Jack. He lived with his mother and they were very poor. All they had in the world was one cow. One morning, Jack's mother told him to take their cow to the market to sell her.

On the way to the market, Jack met a **strange** man. He offered him some **magic** beans in exchange for the cow. Jack took the beans and went back home. When

Jack's mother saw the beans she was very angry and said, "You have been **tricked**," and threw the beans out of the window.

The next morning, Jack looked out of the window. There was a giant beanstalk reaching far up into the sky! Jack decided he could solve the **problem** if he went outside and climbed up the beanstalk. He climbed up to the sky and through the clouds, where he saw a **beautiful**

castle and went inside. Once inside, he heard a voice. "Fee, fi, fo, fum!" it bellowed. Jack hid under the table and peeped out. An **enormous** giant came into the room and sat down. On the table, Jack could see a hen and a golden harp. "Lay!" said the giant. The hen laid an egg. The egg was made of gold! "Sing!" said the giant. The harp began to sing. Soon the giant fell asleep. Jack jumped up and left the castle. On his way, he took the hen and the harp.

Suddenly, the harp sang, "Help, master!" With this, the giant woke up and shouted, "Fee, fi, fo, fum!" Jack ran and started climbing down the beanstalk. The giant came down after him. The boy shouted, "Mummy, help!" Luckily, Jack's mother heard him. She took an axe and **chopped** down the beanstalk. The giant fell and crashed to the ground. Nobody ever saw him again. With the golden eggs and the **magic** harp, Jack and his mother were never poor again and lived happily ever after.

Look at them **flit**

Lickety-split

Wiggling

Wiggling

Swerving

Curving

Hurrying

Scurrying

Chasing

Racing

Whizzing

Whisking

Flying

Frisking

Tearing around

With a **leap** and a **bound**

But none of them making the tiniest

tiniest

tiniest

tiniest

tiniest

sound

A poor, **foolish** woodcutter and his wife had two children, a boy and a girl, named Hansel and Gretel. Their mother died when they were young and Hansel and Gretel were very sad. Soon their father remarried, but their stepmother was very **cruel** and **selfish**. One day, she took the children deep into the forest and left them there. But clever Hansel had some breadcrumbs in his pocket and had dropped them on the way so that they could find their way back home. Alas! The birds had eaten all the crumbs and they couldn't find the path that led back home.

So, **brave** Hansel and Gretel went deeper and deeper into the forest. They were both hungry and tired. Finally, after walking for a long time, they came across a beautiful cottage made of chocolate, candies and cake. "Look, Hansel! A chocolate brick!" shouted Gretel in delight, and they both ate it hungrily.

But they hadn't realised that a **wicked** witch lived in the cottage. She had seen Hansel and Gretel and wanted to eat them. She grabbed

Hansel and locked him in a cage. The **lazy** witch forced Gretel to do all the cleaning work in the cottage. She had decided to eat Hansel first and wanted to make a soup out of him. The witch began boiling a huge pot of water for the soup, when Gretel crept up behind her and gave the **wicked** witch a mighty push from behind. The **wicked** witch fell into the boiling water, disappeared and was never seen again!

Hansel and Gretel found the witch's treasure in the cottage and carried it home with them. Their **nasty** stepmother had died while they were lost, and their **kind** father welcomed them back with tears of joy. They never went hungry again!

Then suddenly the King saw the great straggling, **sprawling**, wicked shape of the Red Dragon. And he knew what he must do.

He picked up The Book of Beasts and jumped on the back of the **gentle** Hippogriff, and leaning down he whispered in its ear: "Fly, dear Hippogriff, fly your very fastest to the Pebbly Waste."

And when the Dragon saw them, it turned and flew after them, with its great red wings.

But the Dragon could not catch the Hippogriff. Its red wings were bigger than the Hippogriff's white ones, but they were not so strong, and so the white-winged horse flew further ahead, still **pursued** by the dragon, until it reached the very middle of the Pebbly Waste, which was made up of **loose, shifting** stones, and there was no grass there and no trees.

The Dragon **appeared** but the sun was too hot for the Dragon. Its flying was very **feeble** and

it was looking around everywhere for a tree, for the sun was **shining** like a gold coin in the blue sky, and there was not a tree for a hundred miles.

The white-winged horse flew around and around the Dragon as it **writhed** on the dry pebbles. It was getting very hot: indeed, parts of it even had begun to smoke. It knew that it would catch fire in another minute unless it could get under a tree. It **snatched** with its red claws at the King and Hippogriff, but it was too **feeble** to reach them.

Once upon a time there lived a kind, **polite** princess with **fair** skin and blue eyes. She was so **fair** that she was named Snow White. Her mother died when she was a baby and her father married again. This queen was very beautiful but she was also very cruel. This wicked, **rotten** stepmother wanted to be the most beautiful lady in the kingdom. She would often ask her magic mirror, "Mirror! Mirror on the wall! Who is the fairest of them all?" And the magic mirror would say, "You are, Your Majesty!" But one day, the mirror replied, "Snow White is the fairest of them all!"

The **boastful** queen was very angry and jealous of Snow White. She ordered her huntsman to take Snow White into the forest and kill her, but when the huntsman reached the forest, he took pity on Snow White and instead set her free.

When it was daylight, Snow White came across a tiny cottage and went inside. There was nobody there, but she found seven plates on the table and seven tiny beds in the bedroom. She cooked a delicious meal and cleaned the house, but grew tired and fell asleep on one of the tiny beds. At night, the seven dwarfs who lived in the cottage came home and found Snow White sleeping on the bed.

When she woke up, at first they were **bashful**, as she was so beautiful, but she told them her story and the seven dwarfs asked her to stay with them. When the dwarfs were away, Snow White would make delicious meals for them. The dwarfs loved her and cared for her. Every morning, when they left the house, they instructed her never to open the door to strangers.

Meanwhile, in the palace, the wicked queen asked again, "Mirror! Mirror on the wall! Who is the fairest of them all?"

20 Snow White and the Seven Dwarfs

The mirror replied, "Snow White is the fairest of them all. She lives with the seven dwarfs in the woods!" The wicked stepmother was so furious that she made a poisonous potion and dipped a shiny red apple into it. She disguised herself as an old peasant woman and went into the woods with the apple to trick Snow White. She offered Snow White the apple while she was collecting firewood because she was **stubborn** and determined to go out to help the dwarfs, even though it wasn't safe for her. **Trusting** Snow White took a bite of the apple and fell into a deep sleep. The wicked stepmother went back to the palace and asked the mirror, "Mirror! Mirror on the wall! Who is the fairest of them all?" The mirror replied, "You are, Your Majesty!" and she was very happy.

When the seven dwarfs came home to find Snow White lying on the floor, they were very upset. They cried all night and showed how **tender** they were to Snow White by carefully building her a glass coffin. They kept the coffin in front of the cottage. One day, **proud** Prince Charming was going past the cottage and he saw Snow White lying in the coffin. He said to the dwarfs, "My! My! She is so beautiful! I would like to kiss her!" And he did. Immediately, Snow White opened her eyes. She was alive again! The Prince and the **jolly** seven dwarfs were very happy. Prince Charming married Snow White and took her to his palace and lived happily ever after.

They came like **dewdrops overnight**

Eating every plant in sight,

Those **nasty** worms with legs that crawl

So **creepy** up the garden wall,

Green **prickly fuzz** to hurt and **sting**

Each **unsuspecting living** thing.

How I hate them! Oh, you know

I'd love to **squish** them with my toe.

But then I see past their **disguise**,

Someday they'll all be butterflies.

Once upon a time there lived a good king and his queen. They had no children for many years and were very sad.

Then, one day, the queen gave birth to a lovely baby girl and the whole **kingdom** was happy. There was a grand celebration and all the fairies in the kingdom were invited. But the king forgot to invite an old fairy. She came to the celebrations but was very angry. The good fairies all wished the baby well, but the **evil** fairy gave her a bad **wish.**

"When the baby is sixteen, she will touch a spindle, and die!" The king and queen were shocked, and begged the fairy to forgive them and take her words back, but the fairy refused to do so.

The other fairies said, "We cannot undo what the old fairy has spoken. But we certainly can make it different. Your child shall not die when she touches the spindle. But she will fall, with everyone in the **palace,** into a deep sleep for a hundred years. Then, a prince will come along and wake her up." Hearing this, the king and the queen were relieved. The king forbade everyone from spinning so that the princess would never touch a spindle.

The princess grew up to be a kind girl. When she was sixteen years old, she was walking in the palace and found a room she had never seen before. She went in and saw an old lady spinning.

"What is this? May I try?" she asked. The old lady said, "Of course, my pretty little child!" And the princess sat down to spin. But the moment she touched the spindle, she fell to the floor in a deep slumber. The whole palace fell asleep. For a hundred years, they all slept soundly.

A hundred years passed. There came a **gallant** prince from a far-off land. He went deep into the forest and crossed many rivers and then came across the **forgotten** and **enchanted** palace. He had come to the sleeping kingdom and was amazed a tall forest had grown up. It was like a **maze** to get to the castle gates. The guards, the servants, the cats and the cows were all fast asleep and snoring.

The prince then found the sleeping princess. She was such a beautiful girl that the prince kissed her. The princess yawned and opened her eyes. She saw the prince and smiled. She asked him, "Are you my prince?" Everyone woke up and the prince married the princess. They lived **happily ever after.**

The crocodile, with **cunning** smile, sat in the dentist's chair.

He said, "Right here and everywhere my teeth **require repair**."

The dentist's face was turning white. He **quivered, quaked** and **shook**.

He muttered, "I suppose I'm going to have to take a look."

"I want you," Crocodile declared, "to do the back ones first.

The molars at the very back are easily the worst."

He opened wide his massive jaws. It was a **fearsome** sight –

At least three hundred pointed teeth, all sharp and shining white.

The dentist kept himself well clear. He stood two yards away.

He chose the longest **probe** he had to search out the decay.

"I said to do the *back ones* first!" the Crocodile called out.

"You're much too far away, dear sir, to see what you're about.

To do the back ones properly you've got to put your head

Deep down inside my great big mouth," the grinning Crocky said.

The poor old dentist wrung his hands and, weeping in **despair**,

He cried, "No no! I see them all extremely well from here!"

Just then, in burst a lady, in her hands a golden chain.

She cried, "Oh Croc, you naughty boy, you're playing tricks again!"

"Watch out!" the dentist shrieked and started climbing up the wall.

"He's after me! He's after you! He's going to eat us all!"

"Don't be a twit," the lady said, and flashed a gorgeous smile.

"He's **harmless**. He's my little pet, my lovely crocodile."

The two children stood in the gathering darkness. There was no way home. Their father had left them there; **abandoned** them in the **creepy** woods, and they were **lost.** Gretel was furious. "What a mean thing to do!" she muttered. "Our dad is the worst dad in the whole world."

Hansel nodded. Gretel was right; she was always right.

"Well!" said Gretel, "We will have to sort this out ourselves," and she stamped off down one of the paths with her brother, Hansel, running after. "Aren't you afraid?" he called.

"No time to be afraid," replied Gretel. "We need somewhere to sleep."

The children walked along the **winding** path beneath the **looming** trees until they saw a glimmer in the distance. "There appears to be a

flashing light. How strange," **murmured** Gretel. Soon the children were at the edge of a clearing, and in the clearing, there was a beautiful cottage covered in glittering, sparkling decorations. Just as Gretel stepped up to knock at the door, it was flung open and loud music **boomed** out.

A tiny man looked up at the children. "Do you like to dance?" he asked. "We are having a party. Our friend Snow White and her friend Red have come to visit and we are **celebrating.** Do come in."

The children stepped into the noisy room and saw an **incredible** sight: streamers and bunting, tables piled with **scrumptious** food, disco lights and so many people! There were seven small men all dressed in bright colours, a girl in a red hood, a girl with jet black hair, a wolf, a woodcutter and a granny. Everyone was chatting and dancing and having a wonderful time.

"I think we have found a new home," said Gretel. "I told you we could sort this out." And Hansel just nodded. Gretel was right, as usual.

The Owl and the Pussy-cat went to sea

    In a beautiful **pea green** boat,

They took some honey, and **plenty** of money,

    Wrapped up in a five-pound note.

The Owl looked up to the stars above,

    And sang to a small guitar,

"O lovely Pussy! O Pussy, my love,

What a beautiful Pussy you are,

       You are,

       You are!

What a beautiful Pussy you are!"

Pussy said to the Owl, "You **elegant fowl**!

    How **charmingly** sweet you sing!

O let us be married! Too long we have tarried:

    But what shall we do for a ring?"

They sailed away, for a year and a day,

    To the land where the Bong-Tree grows

And there in a wood a Piggy-wig stood

With a ring at the end of his nose,

       His nose,

       His nose,

With a ring at the end of his nose.

"Dear Pig, are you **willing** to sell for one shilling

    Your ring?" Said the Piggy, "I will."

So they took it away, and were married next day

    By the Turkey who lives on the hill.

They **dined** on mince, and **slices** of quince,

    Which they ate with a runcible spoon;

And hand in hand, on the **edge** of the sand,

    They danced by the light of the moon,

       The moon,

       The moon,

They danced by the light of the moon.

The Weasel by Ted Hughes

The Weasel **whizzes** through the woods, he sizzles through the brambles,
Compared to him a rabbit **hobbles** and a whippet ambles.

He's all the heads of here and there, he spins you in a **dither**,
He's peering out of everywhere, his ten tails **hither** and thither.

The Weasel never waits to **wonder** what it is he's after.
It's **butchery** he wants, and BLOOD, and **merry belly** laughter.

That's all, that's all, it's no good thinking he's a darling **creature**.
Weight for weight he's twice a tiger, which he'd like to teach you.

A lucky thing we're giants! It can't be very nice
Dodging from the Weasel down the **mazes** of the mice.

Growing the plants

Tomato plants are **sub-tropical** and need lots of sunlight and rich **fertile** soil to grow. Tomato plants need to be **sown** in a seed tray first and then, once they have grown into little **seedlings**, they can be planted in a pot. The sowing time is January to March and the planting time is between May and June. The tomato fruits can be harvested and eaten anytime between July and September.

Once the fruit is setting in well, they need a large amount of water: 12 litres per plant each week. These also need a **liquid** comfrey feed.

Pests

Whitefly are the most likely pest to affect the tomatoes and these can be **harmful**. The adult flies (they look like tiny moths) lay eggs on the underside of leaves. The growing eggs feed on the leaves, leaving a sticky secretion which attracts other diseases. As soon as you see the eggs, try spraying with water to wash them off, and remove the rest by hand; this will **protect** the plants.

Harvesting

Pick as soon as the fruits are **ripe** (colour and size will identify this) for the best flavour – eat as soon as possible. Hopefully, there will be a lovely crop of tomatoes. Picking the tomatoes also encourages the production of more fruit. As soon as a frost threatens in October/ November, **harvest** all the fruit immediately and ripen them on a window sill.

The fresh-picked tomatoes should last longer on the kitchen counter than supermarket-bought ones, which are probably a few days old when you get them.

What **wondrous** life is this I lead!
Ripe apples drop about my head;
The **luscious** clusters of the **vine**
Upon my mouth do **crush** their wine;
The nectarine and **curious** peach
Into my hands themselves do reach;
Stumbling on melons, as I pass,
Ensnared with flowers, I fall on grass.

Here at the **fountain's** sliding foot,
Or at some fruit-tree's **mossy** root,
Casting the body's vest aside,
My soul into the boughs does glide;
There, like a bird, it sits and sings,
Then whets and combs its silver wings,
And, til prepared for longer flight,
Waves in its **plumes** the various light.

Persephone and the Pomegranate Seeds by Geraldine McCaughrean

Background

Zeus, king of the gods, had two brothers and three sisters. Each had an important job. One of his sisters, Demeter, was in charge of the harvest. If Demeter did not do her job, the crops could die, and everyone would starve. It was important to keep Demeter happy.

Demeter had a daughter, Persephone, and she really loved her. They played together in the fields almost every day. All the crops grew well and the flowers grew everywhere.

Pluto, the king of the underworld, decided he loved Persephone and he kidnapped her and took her back to the underworld.

Meanwhile, up on Earth, Demeter came looking for her daughter at the end of the day.

"Persephone darling! Time to go home!"

But there was no answer. Demeter called out and asked everyone she met, but it was **hopeless**. Persephone had simply **disappeared**.

All Demeter's work was forgotten as she **searched** high and low for the child. Nothing mattered but to find Persephone. So the flowers **wilted**. The crops stopped growing. And as Demeter **wept**, the trees wept with her, shedding their leaves in brown and yellow tears.

After searching the world over, Demeter returned to Sicily and sat down in **despair** beside a river. As she **gazed** at the water, what should come spinning by on the current but a little cord of flowers.

"Persephone is in the Underworld," whispered the water. "I saw her! Pluto has **stolen** her away to be his queen."